"As someone with forty years of experience and Grandma status, I thoroughly appreciated *The Strategic Grandparent* book. It contains practical wisdom, helpful tools, and personal examples that make it both relatable and relevant. Now more than ever in the church, youth ministry must move from programs and events run by 'experts' to relationships of mentoring and discipling. This book invites grandparents to step confidently into their unique role of influence and love with the young people in their lives."

—**Debbie Herbeck**, founder and director of Pine Hills Girls' Camp and founder and executive director of the Be Love Revolution, a ministry for young women. She is the author of *Safely through the Storm: 120 Reflections on Hope*, *Firmly on the Rock: 120 Reflections on Faith*, and *Love Never Fails: 120 Reflections on Love*. Debbie and her, husband, Peter live in Ann Arbor, Michigan, and are the parents of four young adult children and seven grandchildren.

MICHAEL SHAUGHNESSY

THE STRATEGIC
GRANDPARENT

YOUR MOST IMPORTANT (AND FUN) ROLE YET

Published by The Word Among Us Press
7115 Guilford Drive, Suite 100
Frederick, Maryland 21704
wau.org

24 23 22 21 20   1 2 3 4 5

ISBN: 978-1-59325-391-2
eISBN: 978-1-59325-392-9

Unless otherwise noted, Scripture texts in this work are taken from
The Catholic Edition of the Revised Standard Version of the Bible,
copyright © 1965, 1966 National Council of the Churches of Christ
in the United States of America. Used by permission.
All rights reserved worldwide.

Excerpts from the English translation of the *Catechism of
the Catholic Church* for use in the United States of America,
Second Edition, copyright © 1997, by the United States Catholic
Conference—Libreria Editrice Vaticana. Used with permission.

Cover design by Suzanne Earl

Made and printed in the United States of America

Library of Congress Control Number: 2020905572

A PRAYER FOR GRANDPARENTS

Lord Jesus, you were born of the Virgin Mary, the daughter of Saints Joachim and Anne.
Look with love on grandparents the world over.
Protect them! They are a source of enrichment for families, for the Church and for all of society.
Support them! As they grow older, may they continue to be for their families strong pillars of Gospel faith, guardians of noble domestic ideals, living treasuries of sound religious traditions.
Make them teachers of wisdom and courage, that they may pass on to future generations the fruits of their mature human and spiritual experience.

Lord Jesus, help families and society to value the presence and role of grandparents.
May they never be ignored or excluded, but always encounter respect and love.
Help them to live serenely and to feel welcomed in all the years of life which you give them.
Mary, Mother of all the living, keep grandparents constantly in your care, accompany them on their earthly pilgrimage, and by your prayers, grant that all families may one day be reunited in our heavenly homeland, where you await all humanity for the great embrace of life without end. Amen!

—**Pope Benedict XVI**

CONTENTS

PREFACE

I began Grandly, The Strategic Grandparents Club in order to offer grandparents a new and somewhat different approach to passing on their faith to their grandchildren.

Grandly recognizes that the relationships you have with your sons, daughters, and their spouses—the parents of your grandchildren—affect the way you can work with your grandchildren. Sometimes you are on the same page, and other times you are not. The state of those relationships has a significant impact on what you can do. There are books that will help you build, repair, restore, and strengthen your relationships with your children. This isn't one of those books.

I assume that the grandparents reading this understand the complexity of those relationships and, at times, are flummoxed by them. But even in the most complex relationships, there is still a lot that grandparents can do.

Obviously, the primary responsibility for teaching your grandchildren belongs to their parents. Your role as a grandparent clearly depends on what they are doing, what they are happy about you doing, and what they might oppose. That will vary by family, by parent, by child, and by season. Generally speaking, everyone can find some things to agree on for the good of the young. Few people are actually against politeness, patience, honesty, and most other virtues.

In this book, I've included many examples of effective strategic grandparenting, each from a real situation. The fact that these strategies were effective in their particular settings does not mean they will be effective in all situations or at all times. Many of the examples can be adapted, however, and all of them demonstrate the rich opportunities for strategic grandparenting.

I don't always distinguish what I mean by youth. Sometimes the age of a child can be determined by the context. Sometimes I use the words "infant," "child," "tween," "teen," and "young adult" because the example fits a particular age. Sometimes age doesn't matter. Once again, the point isn't to give you a blueprint to follow: "Just do this; it always works." My hope is to inspire you to do the right thing, whatever that may be.

My aim, in this book, is to introduce you to strategic grandparenting to help you to play your God-given, unique role in your grandchildren's lives. God has equipped you with faith, hope, and love to help you think, pray, and act strategically. By his grace and your efforts, your grandchildren may become excellent Christians, fine citizens, and the persons God intends them to become.

The first chapter of this book, "What If?," notes the need for hope in order to engage the mission of passing on your faith to your grandchildren. It puts together two things seldom thought to go together: grandparenting and youth work. It's the perfect partnership.

Chapter 2 highlights what grandparents uniquely bring to that partnership.

Chapter 3 is a crash course on the knowledge and skills of youth workers as they work with young people today: Youth Ministry 101.

Chapter 4 is about equipping grandparents to become strategic in how they think, pray, and act.

The book ends with a call: "If you are going to do grandparenting, do it GRANDLY!"

Mike Shaughnessy

January 26, 2020, the feast of St. Timothy, the grandson of Lois. May such grandparents and their grandchildren change the world again.

ACKNOWLEDGMENTS

I would like to thank the following people:

- Bill Navarre, the first strategic grandparent I knew.
- Pili Galvan de Abouchaar, the first director of Grandly, who made an idea become a reality.
- Beth McNamara, who charmed me, against my better judgment, to write this book.
- All of the youth whom I have been privileged to serve since I began doing youth work, first in St. Cloud, Avon, and Minneapolis, Minnesota, and then London, Munich, Belfast, Ann Arbor, Lansing, and too many other sites to count in North America.
- Those with whom I have served in youth work, especially my sister Carmen, who has promoted Grandly as youth ministry, round two.
- The staff of Young Life, University Christian Outreach, Youth Initiatives, St. Paul's Outreach, and Kairos.
- The staff and supporters of Grandly, The Strategic Grandparents Club, especially our copy editor Kris Whitaker; the authors who wrote articles that appear in this book; and the donors who sustain this mission.
- My parents and grandparents, who were great role models.
- The Servants of the Word, my brothers.

I have changed the names of many of the people in this book, as well as the details in some of the stories, to protect the privacy of contributors.

CHAPTER 1

WHAT IF?

"Sigh."
—Charlie Brown, on turning seventy, October 30, 2016.

Imagine the comic strip *Peanuts* with all of those fascinating characters now in their seventies! Charlie Brown is sitting at that outdoor psychiatric office of Lucy van Pelt: the doctor is IN. Charlie is looking at his smartphone, worried that Google can read his mind, and says, "Do you think Google knows what I'm thinking?" Lucy, the same as ever, responds, "Charlie, no one cares what you're thinking! Five cents, please."

Good grief!

We all have a little Charlie Brown inside of us.

Maybe a new wave of despair crashes over us as we see the latest unbelievable trend in youth culture. Maybe it's a new pop song using four-letter words, or a documentary on the rising rate of suicide among preteens, or a YouTube video on how to get revenge on an ex-boyfriend. Maybe it is another statistic about how young people are leaving the Church, or becoming more self-centered, or distracted by social media.

"Sigh."

I have a lot of friends who are grandparents. The vast majority of them are concerned about the spiritual welfare of their grandchildren but feel helpless to do much. Some of them have grandchildren who are barely trained in basic morality: honesty, unselfishness, reliability, and kindness. Others have tweens who don't know the Lord's Prayer yet. They have never been to church, and their only understanding of Jesus comes from mall music at Christmas. They put Jesus Christ in the same category as Santa Claus, Frosty the Snowman, and Bing Crosby.

"*Sigh.*"

Should you be surprised by that reaction? No, not if you remember your grandparents doing the same thing when the Beatles were on The Ed Sullivan Show. They thought the world was going mad.

We sigh. Why?

We sigh when we lose hope. Despair is a natural *reaction* to distress, but giving up is the wrong *response*. Hope, that mysterious Christian virtue, is what's needed instead.

Hope

Whenever I train youth workers to give talks to youth, I ask them to express different emotions without words. Inevitably, when I ask them to express discouragement, they sigh or bow their heads. Then I ask them to express hope and determination. What do you think they do? They inhale deeply. They flex their muscles.

When we lose hope, we become dispirited. Our spirit is deflated. When we gain hope, the opposite happens. Our spirit expands: we inhale; we are inspired; we are buoyed up. More than a pleasant disposition, hope is assurance, especially when we face something that would normally disappoint us.

If there is one thing you get from this book, I hope it is hope.

Hope is a theological virtue. It is a grace, a gift from God. Our hope is in the Lord, the omniscient, omnipotent, all-loving God. He knows what to do, has the power to do it, and has the love that ensures good, not evil, will result. We can be "up" because we know the Lord will act in a timely fashion. "Happy is he whose help is the God of Jacob, / whose hope is in the LORD his God" (Psalm 146:5).

What is real hope? It is motivation, inspiration. It is YES in the times of Ugh!

Hope is not optimism. Optimism helps me think I can win. It identifies the outcome I wish to see. It's like a Disney movie. A child gazes up into the sky, rubs a lamp, makes a wish, and it all comes true. That "up"-timism isn't Christian hope. It might make a great fairy tale, but it is not hope. Christian hope isn't dreamy. Christian hope gives me the strength to fight against the odds.

Hope is more than a pleasant disposition. Hope is assurance, a sense of certainty—certainty based on the truth that God reigns, that he is good, and that all things will work out for the good of those who believe in Jesus Christ. And hope, when placed in God, does not disappoint us.

False hope does disappoint. Whenever our hope is anchored in our dreams, we are setting ourselves up for disappointment.

God does not guarantee our dreams or best wishes. He guarantees his love and his help.

As unfortunate as it is, our grandchildren can make bad choices. If one of them decides not to follow the Lord or is leading a disastrous life, it can be devastating. Yet it is in exactly these times that we need hope—real hope. Hope reminds us that God's love for our grandchildren far exceeds our own. So do his power and his wisdom. God has not abandoned our grandchildren. He will do everything to win them, and he will never dismiss our prayers for them. This hope doesn't fail.

No situation is hopeless in the eyes of God. All Christians, sinners and saints, have good and bad chapters in their lives. Look at Peter, Paul, and Mary Magdalene: If we had seen any of them at the wrong time, we might have written them off as cowards, murderers, cheats, liars, and lunatics, but then God rescued them.

Peter would not have inspired your confidence if your first encounter with him was when he was vehemently denying he knew the Lord. Mary Magdalene had seven demons besetting her and probably wouldn't have been anyone's best friend forever. Paul was actively persecuting the early leaders of the Church and putting some of them to death. What Christian would have put him on their short list of potentially great saints?

Or just reflect on your own life. Who among us hasn't been ashamed at some point? Would you want that moment to be the one for which you are remembered? Yet God, in his mercy, didn't abandon you. He probably rescued you more than once. God has a good track record! Our hope is anchored in him, not in luck, in things going our way, not in our best laid plans.

Hope helps us hang in there. "This story is not over yet!"

It takes time to gain the mature hope grandparents have. It comes with the long-term view that grows decade by decade. Mature hope sees that we can help a new generation gain the human and spiritual skills to build something new, strong, and holy—something that will last, something that will be there to support generations to come. It takes a long-term view to plant a forest, build a new culture, or even reroof Notre Dame Cathedral.

During the fifteen years I lived in Europe, I toured many of the great cathedrals. I was struck over and over again by their majesty. These monuments to the glory of God took centuries to build and still inspire awe today. How did our ancestors do it? Building a wall, a support pillar, or a roof was not easy without modern tools. It took patience and sweat. The detail we can still see in a piece of stone that was carved six hundred years ago is amazing. Some mason spent hours carving the curly wool on the ear of a stone sheep. A slip of the hand or a faulty piece of stone and a week's worth of work could be easily lost, but these people were dedicated to the idea that their labor of love would serve future generations. They stayed on task.

The founding fathers of these cathedrals rallied the whole community to a vision that would need buy-in from multiple generations. The first years were spent simply laying the floor and foundations. The fathers taught their sons and the mothers taught their daughters what to do. Eventually, as "grand-founders," many taught their grandsons and granddaughters the skills they needed. The hand-carved woodwork, the hand-painted art, and the hand-blown glass we see today are still beautiful, and the hands that created them were often trained by the wisest and most skilled—the grandparents.

A few of the grand-founders might have lived long enough to become great-grand-founders. Even then, they never lived to see the cathedral finished. They didn't need to. They had hope. The "grand"-aged people have always been a sturdy foundation upon which the future rested.

The same is true of the family today. We began a work in raising one generation as parents, and now we have the opportunity to pass on faith, skill, and virtue to our grandchildren. We are not building with brick and mortar. We are building with living stones and making saints for the kingdom of God.

Grandparents and grandchildren are the two arms of a "building" strategy. Grandparents have hope and their grandchildren are the incarnation of that hope. They will be the foundations of future good things. Grandparents build anew when they see this truth and act with hope—not with the sweat of their brows or the strength of their backs, but with the power of the long-term view, a deep hope. They understand that what they do in their old age may be more fruitful than many things they did when they were young and vigorous. They are older and wiser. They know what fails and what succeeds better than they did when they were thirty-five. What you give to your grandchildren now might take sixty years to mature, but that's OK.

Who knows what our grandchildren will do or be in this life for God's glory? We may never see those results in our lifetime. We certainly will be tempted to think our contribution is small and doesn't matter, but when we give what we can with love, it does make a difference. Building the kingdom of God is a multigenerational task. It was the same with the great cathedrals. We must do what we can, and let God use that for his purposes, trusting we will see the results someday from above the clouds.

A Dangerous Freedom

God runs the universe differently than I would: he gives us freedom right out of the womb. I wouldn't! If it were up to me, I would rig the system. I would make people choose what I deemed good, and I would not give them any choice about it until they were at least twenty-six. Consider how many bad choices could be avoided with my approach.

But God gives us a fearful level of freedom. He allows us to shape our temporal and eternal destiny, and, in doing so, he dignifies us greatly. He has not given such dignity to anything else on earth. Most of creation, a rock, for example, has no choice.

Rock one: "I'm thinking we should just sit here for another millennium."

Rock two: "Thinking? What's that?"

Even the higher mammals do not have the ability to choose as we do. I used to have a dog, and though she could choose to chase a squirrel or a rabbit, she did not have the ability to reason and express that choice.

"Squirrel or rabbit? Well, I had squirrel for lunch yesterday, and I may want to save another one for the winter. Sorry, rabbit."

My dog didn't know how to think through her actions, and even if she did, she didn't sit on the porch afterward and bark her wisdom to her puppies. A horse cannot lie to its rider. Can an ape ask, "Why do I exist?"

We, on the other hand, make decisions about good and evil every day. Not only are we born with a fearful freedom, as we get older that freedom becomes more powerful. As a baby, I had little power to reject my parents. Did you ever run away from home? I did when I was seven. I made it next door for about half an hour. By the time I was eighteen, I chose what college I would attend, and I was responsible for my own tuition. I was making adult decisions. I had friends who made some very bad decisions that had significant long-term consequences, and I would make some of my own decisions differently today. Fortunately, God continued to guide me and give me help.

I have seen a lot in my many years as a youth worker, and I have learned that everyone's story is different. Some are beautiful, gradually unfolding stories of increasing faith, hope, and love. Some are heart-stopping roller-coaster rides.

I watched a young girl with a delightful personality, from a good family, grow up over the past fifteen years. I went to her Confirmation, saw her respond on retreats, witnessed her serve in her youth group, and then saw her hook up with the wrong young man and become an unwed mother at eighteen. She had no money, no job, and no high school diploma. It was heartbreaking for her parents, but the story isn't finished yet. Here is what she wrote about her current reality and posted on our website for grandparents:

I am a young mom. When I was eighteen, I gave birth to my son, Mark. I was unmarried and unequipped to manage my own life, let alone a child's. At the same time, I was suddenly confronted with the overwhelming privilege of motherhood and greatly desired to raise my son well. I spent much of the next five years living with my parents. They walked side by side with me in raising Mark. In order to live with them, my parents required me to go to church. It wasn't what I would have chosen, but it was part of the package.

Needless to say, "Grandma" had not planned on this chapter in her life either. However, she embraced this time and the opportunity to share her faith with her grandson. She taught Mark to say prayers and pay attention in church. Now, at age five, he takes the initiative in saying grace before meals. She signed him up for religious education and paid for his classes. Mark loves it! He comes home and tells me what he's learned and retells the Bible stories.

My mother's biggest impact on Mark has come from talking about her own faith. "Do you know how much we love you? Do you know how much God loves you? He loves you so much he has put all these wonderful people in your life to love you!"

My mother and Mark seem to have developed a common "lost and found" bond! Whenever she loses something, she prays aloud for help. If Mark loses something, she asks, "Did you pray?" Now, when Mark loses something, he prays, and when he finds it, he says, "Thank you, Jesus!"

Why am I writing this story for grandparents? My mother, Mark's grandmother, was one of the first people impacted by Grandly, The Strategic Grandparents Club. Its message of hope and the idea that she could be entering one of the most important times of her life for sharing her faith struck her as true, and she acted on it in Mark's life, but that's her story.

As for me, my story is still developing, but it certainly, already, has a theme in it for grandparents: Don't give up hope on your stumbling children. We might be stumbling over the rock of our salvation.

This young woman's story is not uncommon today, but notice—the challenging situation itself is becoming her path back home to faith. That gives me hope.

God, being good, doesn't offer us just one shot at eternal life. He quietly works (often through other human beings) to help us choose whether we want to be with him for all eternity or not. So we should never give up hope. God has more options than we can imagine to win the fight for our grandchildren.

God's Options

What if one of God's best options is you?

"*Me?*"

"*Yes, you.*"

There is a grandmother in the New Testament, Lois, who could have taken the give-up approach with her grandson, Timothy: "The Romans run the world. They are pagans.

Caesar is a tyrant. Our children are being deluded. The faith of our fathers is being lost. They don't keep the feasts. Moses is getting rebranded. No one knows the Ten Commandments anymore, and our priests are all self-centered, two-faced, and sanctimonious. Why bother anyway?" She could have given up, but she didn't. She was a key player in her grandson's life, so much so that St. Paul wrote to Timothy and reminded him of the critical role she had played in his early life (see 2 Timothy 1:5). She was the right person, at the right time, in the right role.

So was my grandfather.

Sixty years ago, I had a conversation with him. I doubt that either of us would have put it in our top ten conversations ever. My grandfather was born in America in the 1890s and spoke German until his first day of school. He remained fluent and worked as a translator during World War I. When I was going into fourth grade, my school offered classes in foreign languages. (Neither of my parents had learned one, but I decided to ask Grandpa if I should.) We had a conversation which could be summarized as, "Jawohl! Learn German."

So I began. I nearly quit studying German in seventh grade but gave up band instead. I intended to quit it again in ninth grade, but my school brought in an excellent new German teacher, so I continued. When I went to college, my German was good enough for me to start upper-level classes as a freshman. I knew I wanted to study theology, but what jobs were there in that field for a twenty-two-year-old? So I did a double major in theology and German.

When I graduated, I became one of the first full-time, lay Catholic youth ministers in Minnesota. Fifteen years later I moved to London, but I worked periodically with youth from guess where? Germany! Why? Because I spoke German. I did Jugendarbeit for a decade before returning to the US.

I had been back for three years when I received a call from one of the German youth I had worked with. She was having a faith crisis. At first, I wasn't sure what to say. She needed some real help, and I knew I couldn't give enough in one phone call. As we spoke, it became clear that she needed to leave behind a set of unhelpful friends and reestablish her faith in a Christian relational environment as a young adult. I was running a gap-year program and proposed that she consider coming to the US. She did, and it transformed her life. When she returned to Germany, she married and ended up living next door to her older brother, who had abandoned his faith. Soon, she was sharing her faith with him, his wife, and their children. They rediscovered their faith and are now active in Christian leadership.

I see a direct line between the casual conversation I had with my grandfather and those two young families in Germany today. My grandfather was used by God in a way he would never know.

God has ways of using grandparents that have huge ripple effects. What if the biggest ripple from your life will come from a conversation you are going to have with one of your grandchildren seven years from now? Think of what ripples might result.

What if God wants to use you to pass on your faith to your grandchildren?

Scratch that what if!

It is a certainty.

> Only take heed, and keep your soul diligently, lest you forget the things which your eyes have seen, and lest they depart from your heart all the days of your life; make them known to your children and your children's children. (Deuteronomy 4:9)

This is a commandment, maybe not one of the ten, but a commandment nonetheless, and one that is reinforced by another that says, "Obey the Lord your God."

The commandment in Deuteronomy—to teach your children and grandchildren what God has done for his people—is one of the most enjoyable commandments you will ever keep. It appears in the Bible within the story of the Exodus—God originally said this to the people who walked through the Red Sea. And they did not forget. In fact, they talked about what they had seen so often that even today we are familiar with the story. Some 3,200 years after the Exodus, we know of God's saving action because those grandparents did their job. They passed on their faith.

You may not have walked through the Red Sea, but you have a faith built on God's action in your life. It's the same God, doing the same thing, and he wants us to do the same thing: pass on our faith.

There is no "what if" here. God hasn't changed his mind. You have been commissioned by God Almighty to do something for him. You haven't merely been recruited by your priest to teach catechism class; you have been assigned by God to pass on your faith to your grandchildren.

Now what if you aren't just commanded, in a general way, like every other grandparent? What if God has an actual plan for how he wants to use you?

The psalmist says,

> My frame was not hidden from thee,
> when I was being made in secret,
> intricately wrought in the depths of the earth.
> Thy eyes beheld my unformed substance;
> in thy book were written, every one of them,
> the days that were formed for me,
> when as yet there was none of them. (Psalm 139:15-16)

What does this mean? Days were formed for you. You were designed by God for your days and your days were selected for you. God made you in secret, intricately, to fulfill a role that only you can play. Some of that role you have completed already, but what if a key part of your role is still in front of you? Indeed, what if the most important thing you will ever do is still in front of you? What if God wants to get you into exactly the right place so you can be a "player" in your grand-daughter's life?

Now let's apply Psalm 139 to your grandchildren rather than you. The same thing is true for them. God created your grandchildren, and he did it with a plan for their lives. He has had them born into this ever-crazy world to fulfill his purposes.

We should not say, "Look at those born in this age. Oh my, how horrible! My poor grandchildren, they will have to live through ugly times."

What if the world is about to get ten times worse than you can imagine? That would mean your grandchildren have been born into one of the most important eras ever. What if your grandchildren are among those who are going to turn it around?

It's time to rethink. You need to get onto the same page as God, right? God has your grandchildren living now because he specifically wants them to make a difference for this age. The question is, how do you get behind God's plans for your grandchildren? How do you help equip them to be those who influence their world for the good? How do you help inspire them? How do you help them see the role they can play? God wants them alive in this age, in this generation, at this time, because he has designed them for a role in this era that only they can play.

Maybe they will be the "kingdom of heaven" builders for their generation. Yes, they will face challenges we never had to face, as we had to face ones our grandparents never had to face. And God is in the middle of it all with them.

Don't let a crazy world steal your hope. You still have something very important to do for people you love deeply. Your grandchildren were born for this age, and you are in a position to equip them to fulfill the role God has for them. What a privilege! You can fill them with hope instead of despair, faith instead of doubt, and love instead of selfishness.

What if the most important thing you will ever do in your entire life is still in front of you?

What if God's main purpose for you isn't yet fulfilled because he wants to use you to pass on your faith to your grandchildren?

What if God has been setting you up your whole life for a role that lies right in front of you now?

The Perfect Partnership

What if God wanted a celibate youth worker to activate grandparents to do youth work? How would he do it? Let me tell you the story.

When I was in high school, I had a conversion experience. Most adults who knew me would not have thought I needed one. I was still an altar server at seventeen. I was getting excellent grades; I didn't smoke, drink, or hang around those who did. Yet one Saturday morning, I read a Christian booklet that a friend had given me. At the end of the booklet, there was a question: Have you ever asked Jesus Christ to be Lord of your life and savior of your soul? After the question, there was a prayer to help the reader do that.

I knew my prayers—the Lord's Prayer, the Rosary, the Creed, the Acts of Faith, Hope, Love, and Contrition—but this was a prayer I had not seen before. I prayed it, and my spiritual life was powerfully transformed. Somehow, I knew God from the inside and not only the outside. My relationship with God became one of the most concrete realities I had ever experienced. Not long thereafter, I decided I wanted to do youth work, to lead other young people into a similar life-changing experience of God.

I went to Saint John's University, a Benedictine school in Collegeville, Minnesota, and volunteered as a youth worker. When I graduated, I was hired as a full-time youth minister in a local parish. In my late twenties, I experienced a further call to remain celibate as part of an ecumenical religious order named the Servants of the Word.

For most of my life, I have been training youth workers and developing strategies and programs for doing more effective youth work. I have always wanted to improve the Church's ability to reach and keep young people, but it hadn't occurred to me that grandparents could play a role very similar to that of a youth worker. When I saw the potential there, I thought, "That's a perfect partnership. What if we helped grandparents do youth work?" Here is how I "saw" it.

I was playing golf a few years ago with a friend, Bill Navarre, a grandfather, and he kept asking me questions about youth. At one point, as we walked to the next tee, he said, "Mike, I think my grandson is ready for a retreat of some sort. Do you have a retreat I could send him on?" We got that to happen and his grandson did great. Bill often tells me about how he is trying to reach his grandchildren with the gospel. He is active in their lives. He has sent them on mission trips and held a family-wide week of prayer and fasting (with great results, but that's another story.) Recently, he told me he purchased a children's audio Bible for another grandson who listens to it on his way to school with his mom.

It struck me that this was a grandfather who thought, prayed, and acted differently than most grandparents I knew. Bill got me thinking: what would happen if other grandparents were this strategic about working with their grandchildren?

But there is another part to the story. I have another friend; let's call him Alex. He and I were in a car together when his wife texted him about their granddaughter's birthday. "Mike," he said, "remind me to stop and get a birthday card for my granddaughter on the way back. We'll probably give her twenty dollars instead of ten. She's becoming a teenager already." And I thought, "That's interesting; there is a real difference between these two grandfathers." Both of them dearly love their grandchildren. One of them thinks strategically about his grandchildren and is having a big impact, and the other one doesn't. He is probably imitating what his grandfather did for him. He had no model and no vision for what he could be doing.

Like most, Alex became a grandparent one day when one of his daughters brought home a newborn baby. He didn't have to go to grandparenting school. He didn't have to get a license. He didn't get any training for the role. He became a grandparent passively, and there was not much that was new to him about caring for a child. He did what he had done before as a parent: changing diapers, bottle-feeding, baby talk. "What's there to learn that I don't already know?" Why would he sign up for a course on grandparenting? What course? There is no PhD program that I know of in grandparenting.

I saw two good grandfathers, but two different approaches. And then my youth-worker brain lit up! One of these guys is strategic and basically doing youth work. What if we trained other grandparents to become strategic about grandparenting and actually taught them some of the skills of youth workers?

What if we recruited grandparents to do youth work? What if we could flood the youth world with grandparents who knew how to do youth work effectively? What if we helped them see that they're not simply, or mainly, substitute moms and dads? They are actually in a very different role. Yes, it is a grandparent's role, but it's also youth work.

I concluded that we needed a more comprehensive view of how youth work should be done—a view that includes grandparents. This could increase the Church's ability to reach and retain the young.

So an idea was conceived: raising up strategic grandparents who could do youth work with their own grandchildren. It's the perfect partnership. What would happen if we were to raise up ten thousand youth workers all over the age of fifty-five who reached three to seven young people each? What would the effect be if we could equip them to be strategic in the lives of their own grandchildren? What if we helped them to learn some basic youth-work principles so they became even more effective in passing on their faith?

But the idea sat for a while. I had a full-time job. I had no one to take on the project and no funding for it. That all changed in July of 2015 when I had a conversation with a young woman named Pili at a youth-work conference in Costa Rica. Pili (Maria del Pilar Abouchaar, née Galván) is now the director of Grandly, The Strategic Grandparents Club.

Pili's Story

I (Pili) am a youth worker, not a grandmother. I can't tell you about being a grandparent, but I can tell you about being a granddaughter.

My grandmother recently turned eighty-one. She has had a huge impact on my life and the lives of her other grandchildren. As long as I can remember (and as long as my parents can remember), she has been a woman of strong faith, really strong morals, and someone who highly values family unity. She has consistently done simple things that demonstrate her faith: always praying before meals, always attending Mass, being generous with her time and other resources, and loving unconditionally, even when it's hard.

I first got the youth-work "bug" after high school, when I did a gap (mission) year in Lansing, Michigan. I returned home, did volunteer youth work during college, graduated, and went off to build my career in industrial engineering. I was still volunteering in youth work, but I knew from my own experience that a good family wasn't enough and a good youth program wasn't enough to help young people live for God. Good peer support through the late teens and early twenties wasn't enough, either. Youth work in the Church still lacked some things, but what?

In July of 2015, I went to an international youth conference in Costa Rica. I bumped into Mike Shaughnessy, who was speaking about being bold in our faith. I had met Mike during the gap year I did in Lansing, so we decided to catch up over lunch. I told him about what I was doing, and then I asked him if he was doing anything new. He started telling me about an idea he had but hadn't yet acted on. "I want to get grandparents doing youth work."

"Wow!" I thought. I had never heard such a radically new approach to youth work. I loved the freshness of the idea and how innovative it was. The more he said, the more I saw a vision for what grandparents could do.

"So this would be a project that activates grandparents to play a key role in young people's lives?" I asked.

"Yes," he said, "by equipping them to think, pray, and act strategically, to move from being passive grandparents to being active, to become the most effective youth workers that youth work has ever seen. But I need someone to make it happen. I can't run the project on the time I have. Would you be interested?"

I knew I had to say, "Yes, tell me more."

Without skipping a beat, he said, "OK, can I turn this lunch into your first job interview?"

That was a shock. I was just having lunch and suddenly I am considering changing my career, moving to a foreign country, working in English, and leaving my family to work with *grandparents on a mission to reach youth in a way that has never been tried before. I was twenty-four.*

I would need a work visa. He would have to find the money to hire me. These were not minor obstacles.

I prayed, thought about it, and I clearly saw God opening doors for me to enter a totally new mission field. That's how Grandly, The Strategic Grandparents Club began—founded by a man in a religious order, with no children or grandchildren, and a young, then-unmarried woman who is serving as its first director.

Let me say something bold here. If I did that as a twenty-four-year-old, you can do youth work at seventy-one.

It took a while to get the start-up funding and the visa, but in December of 2016, we launched Grandly, the perfect partnership of grandparents and youth work.

CHAPTER 2

WHAT YOU ALREADY HAVE

If I had to choose between a great youth worker and a strategic grandparent to influence the young, I would choose the strategic grandparent. Grandparents are uniquely placed to do what no youth worker can do. They have at least six special ingredients that, when mixed with a few youth-work skills, yield a perfect partnership—possibly better than peanut butter and jelly.

In this chapter, let's look at the special ingredients grandparents bring to youth work and why they are uniquely positioned to do that work with their own grandchildren. In the next chapter, we will consider the youth-work skills that can enhance your grandparenting.

Wasting Time on Love

Everyone wastes time now and then, and every grandparent has time to waste. Consider that as we become empty nesters, we gain some time. When we retire, we gain some more. It's not a question of whether or not we will waste time when we get older. The question is on whom or on what we will waste our time. Let's waste it on love. Let's "waste" it on our grand-children. What do I mean by that, exactly?

Ask any youth worker, "What did you do today?" The reply might be, "I played dodgeball with a bunch of ninth-grade boys" or "I hung out at McDonald's with some teenagers after the basketball game."

Youth workers waste a lot of time simply being present to youth. But being there is more than just showing up where young people are. Being there conveys to a young person that their life matters right now. It says, "I am truly interested in your ninth-grade life. Others may be interested in getting you to grow up, to mature, and to excel—often, the faster the bet-ter—but I am interested in you, your thoughts, your feelings, and your goals right now."

That ability to waste time on love is huge. Some youth workers do their job and go home. They might run a good program and put on a successful retreat, but few young peo-ple will point to the youth worker who was just doing his job and say, "He had a big impact on me." However, they will say it to the youth worker who was ready to waste time on them, to be a friend, to attend their volleyball games, or to grab a coke with them. The time wasters will become those whom young people trust and talk to—at times about nothing and at times about the most important things.

Making an investment in relating is more important than ever. Youth are growing up in an increasingly lonely, isolated, and individualistic world. They spend more time on their own, in their room, alone with a screen. The socializing processes of playing and working together are less common, and the effects are documented: increasing depression, suicide, and self-harm. But youth want genuine, stable friends and a real family. They want to be around people who love them, who are interested in them.

So why do they push others away? Because they feel unlovable, not just unloved. They think, "Something is wrong with me!" They don't like that feeling, so they push others away. At other times, they do the exact opposite. They desperately pursue any kind of love relationship they can. Even an abusive friendship is better than no friendship at all. One of the challenges we face when working with youth is understanding what they really want, especially when the signals they are giving confuse us.

In reality, they want to be loved, no matter what they say or do. There are times when they are best left alone, but most of the time, they are actually interested in you breaking down the barriers they have set up, and you should be ready to do it. They were made to love, and the sooner and better they love, the happier they will be. The challenge we face is not whether we should press on through the barriers put up by youth; it is how to do it in a good way.

Interestingly, many times the solution is the same: get into the right position *before* an issue arises. If your grandson experiences you as someone on his side before he needs you on his side, you will find him confiding in you. He will pull away far less often, and even when he does, you will be far more likely to know how to get in close enough to help. That's when you really are a strategic grandparent. You sowed time and are reaping trust.

So waste time on love. It has an impact, maybe not always immediate or obvious, but it has an impact. Even if it doesn't, we should do it because it is right to do. We were created to love.

Presence

Grandparents can be great lovers of youth simply because they can offer love in ways no other adult can. Your presence is different from anyone else's. You have an approachability that other adults don't have.

Other adults are in specific roles that are the primary definers of the relationship. A teacher, a coach, a doctor, or a priest—each fills a role in a child's life. When they come to see your grandchildren, they do so for a reason. You, however, come for no reason at all, and the grandchildren get a hug and a kiss to boot!

You are in a remarkably different position. Grandma isn't a role; it's a person, and a person who is welcoming, reassuring, and always glad to see them. Not even a good youth worker is that welcome.

Your presence also has power.

Jan K., a former youth worker, now grandmother, from Ann Arbor, Michigan, told this story:

Our grandson Mitchell (we call him Mitt) was more like a cat than a fish when it came to water. During his swimming lessons, he was so frightened that he would spend the entire lesson with his arms wrapped around the instructor's neck. We observed that firsthand one day when my husband and I decided to surprise Mitt and showed up at the pool. We watched from behind a glass window as Mitt struggled with his fear of the water while his instructor valiantly attempted to instill confidence in him. It wasn't working.

Then Mitt saw his grandfather looking at him through the window, and in an instant, he changed!

He began to swing his arms into the water and tried to do his best. He didn't instantly swim like a fish, but he did conquer his fear. The awareness of my husband's presence gave Mitt the confidence he needed to believe that he wasn't going to drown. Grandpa was there to save him.

That transformation happened, first, because Grandpa was present. Mitt wouldn't have acquired that confidence if Grandpa had not been there. His presence was necessary. But the other part of what happened is the power of moral authority. The presence of a moral authority gives people reinforcement to overcome timidity and to do the right thing.

Mitt wasn't thinking, "Oooh, I want to be like my grandpa someday." Or "I need to do this to impress Grandpa next time I see him." Mitt drew strength from his grandfather's presence as a moral authority.

Children relate strongly to moral authority. They have learned that some people are trustworthy—such as the police, ministers, doctors, teachers, adult relatives—and others aren't, especially strangers. Your trustworthiness as a grandparent comes from the fact that their main authority, Mom and Dad, signal that you too are a moral authority. Your presence, age, consistency, and track record strengthen that authority.

When you are present, your grandchildren will often up their game. Yes, they want to impress you, but more often they up their game because your presence inspires them to be more than they already are.

Identity

You have fifty or more years of identity formation behind you. You aren't searching for yourself anymore. You aren't wondering what you will be when you grow up. You have a stable identity.

Identity formation is part of the process of growing up. We all went through it: learning about ourselves, establishing what we believe, how we view the world, how we relate to others (or at least we should have).

At our *Do It Grandly* seminar in Maryland, Ryan Petrillo noted an important element of his identity formation when he was young: "My grandmother pursued me. She didn't wait for me to call—she called me. She made an intentional effort for me to get to know her."

Note what he said. She made an intentional effort for *him* to get to know *her*. She flipped the script. She understood the role she could play in connecting Ryan to his own historically rooted identity, and she acted on it. Ryan went on to say how important it was that his faith and identity were rooted in something beyond what he gained from a short-term, cool youth worker. Yes, a youth worker can be an immediate faith model to imitate today, but his grandmother was a faith model that was tested. She was a faith model that was family owned. It was someone whose identity was tied directly, permanently, to his.

When I was growing up, there was a drawing of our family tree on the wall by our dinner table. It went back six generations. Every time we ate together, that drawing served as a reminder of who was who in our family and how we were all related. It provided all of us with a strong sense of identity. Our parents wanted us to know who our ancestors were and where we came from.

One, my great-aunt, had some terrific stories that made me think, "How cool is that?" She told me about the first time she rode in a car, listened to a radio, and saw an airplane. She told me about going to school dances over the snow on a sleigh. She told me about seeing Teddy Roosevelt campaigning for president. She said, "For being a 'bull moose' of a man, he had a high, squeaky voice." On another occasion, it occurred to me that at some point, she might have had a similar conversation about the past with her own grandmother. My great-aunt quite casually said, "Oh, yes. I remember my grandmother telling me where she was when she heard that Abraham Lincoln had been assassinated." That blew me away. I was getting a secondhand account of something that had happened 130 years previously. I was being rooted in history, in my connectedness to significant people and significant events.

Where were you the day President Kennedy was shot? You were alive the day Neil Armstrong walked on the moon. Your grandchildren probably don't know much about 9/11. If you learn to tell these stories from a living perspective, your grandchildren will listen. You will help them be rooted in history. Your history, at least parts of it, is fascinating. Do you know which parts? You have an ancestry, a history, and if you learn to speak of those in an interesting way, your story becomes part of their story.

Some of the best stories you can tell them are about their mom or dad—your own child. Those stories can help your grandchildren learn to honor their father and mother because you have said something honorable about them.

In our highly mobile society, young people have little sense of their family history. The family grave no longer exists. Even the family cemetery has no reality. The young have no village. Their sense of identity is often not deeply rooted in time, location, or relationships.

Also, many youth today have family histories that are not pretty or are virtually unknown. Grandparents can provide a family identity that might otherwise be lacking for grandchildren whose parents' marriage has broken down. Grandparents can be a key part of their grandchildren's stable identity when everything else is free-floating because Grandma and Grandpa are living history—their history.

In a world that overprizes creating one's own identity and being unique, youth are, surprisingly, more interested in belonging to a family than you might expect. I was on a flight to Arizona for Thanksgiving and was seated next to a young man in late high school. I'm a youth worker, so I struck up a conversation with him.

"Are you going home or leaving home?"

"Going to visit my grandma for Thanksgiving."

"Do you live in Detroit?" (That's where we were flying from.)

"Yes, Dearborn."

He was talkative. Over the course of the next twenty minutes, he described his family. He was living with his mom, his sister, and a half brother. He was going to Arizona to be with his dad's side of the family. On that side, he had two married half brothers from his dad's first marriage. He had only met them twice. Plus, he'd be spending time with his dad's third wife, her daughter who was his age, but not a blood relative, and another half brother from his dad's third marriage. Good luck diagraming that family, but it was his!

Only later did I recognize how much he wanted to talk about his family and that, to him, there was nothing odd about his family. It was his. He belonged to a family, and that was important to him.

Your family identity is important, even if it doesn't include anyone great, famous, wealthy, or notable. Your grandchildren belong to that family, even if it is somewhat broken or dispersed. There are always things to be proud of in a young person's family. You probably know what those things are and can help them become rooted in that which is good.

Stability

Teenagers look for role models—usually someone who is young and cool. When I was in junior high school, the older boys who played on the football team wore suit jackets and ties on game days. I couldn't help but admire them and think, "Someday I want to be like them." Their names appeared in the local paper and were the focus of pep rallies. A senior in high school is cool to someone in seventh grade. A junior in college is a great magnet for an eleventh grader. Yes, kids do admire the cool youth worker who is interested in them, who is the model of what they want to be when they get "older," that is to say, twenty-one, or "ancient," like thirty.

I started youth work at twenty. I was one of those cool volunteers (at least I think I was). By the time I was forty, I noticed a change in how youth related to me. I was becoming their fathers' age. It made it harder for them to relate to me, especially if I was friends with their fathers. I had to work harder and longer to build trust. Now that I am more of a grandfatherly age, I notice another change. Young people no longer expect me to react like a parent; they expect me to be more grandfatherly: gentler, less stressed, more stable, and even more trustworthy. In already established relationships such as with my grandnephews and high school kids I know, I have become more easily approachable. In fact, they are somewhat surprised that they can relate so easily to a person my age. They feel more adult around me because I relate to them as I do to adults. They are important and interesting to me.

Cool

You may be the coolest grandma on the block, but you're still not "gucci" (trendy-cool). In fact, a grandparent who is gucci will almost certainly be "sus" (suspicious).

The truth is, you don't even need to know what the current word for "cool" is. Words for cool have a short shelf life, and there is nothing so uncool as people using slang terms for cool that are out-of-date. (Cool still works! Cool has managed to stay cool since it was first used in youth culture in the 1940s.)

Having said that, you can determine almost anyone's age by asking, "What was your slang for cool when you were sixteen?" Awesome, bodacious, brill, chill, cray-cray, crazy, da bomb, epic, fantabulous, far out, fire, fresh, gangsta, gold, groovy, gucci, hellacious (hella), hip hoppin', hot, kickbutt, lit, off da hook, out of sight, peachy, phat, primetime, rad, rockin', savage, sick, smashing, spiffy, sweet, to die for, wet, and wicked. Or as some say now: dope.

But I'm not cool. Youth don't expect Grandma and Grandpa to be cool, to be interested in the latest trends or fashions. Ironically, you become a role model simply because you don't conform. You are above the pressure to fit in. You don't care what other people think. You are independent, and that is an essential quality of cool.

Not long ago, I was talking to a grandmother who was sharing with me how her grandchildren were doing. Some of them were doing well and others were not. She said that some of her grandchildren are struggling with school, some are not going to church, some stopped believing in God, and one has a live-in boyfriend. She was frustrated, overwhelmed, and struggling to maintain hope. In short, she is another grandparent who is tempted to move to Hawaii and forget it all.

But then she said that although she is limited in what she can do, being "limited" doesn't mean there is nothing she can do! All of her grandchildren know who Grandma is, and for her, modeling is the key. They know she has a deep faith in God. They know that she prays and that she prays for each of them. They know that there are certain ways to act when they come to visit her. They know that they don't swear at Grandma's house and that they pray before meals. This is her way of witnessing, by praying for them unconditionally and by simply being who she is around them.

She is a stable moral model. She is rooted and knows what she believes. In the unstable world of youth, she is a rock. The winds blow the chaff away, and she remains. She models commitment.

Commitment is not "in." Young people are afraid to commit. They fear that by choosing one thing, they are likely going to miss out on something else. In the process, they may never commit to anything. But think about it. What instinct or emotion did they follow? Fear! Yes, you can call it fear of missing out (FOMO), but at the end of the day, it is fear.

As grandparents, you have overcome many fears. You have survived. You have learned the value of commitment in spite of whatever has buffeted you. Children can see that. They are perceptive. Your stability and ability to be committed impacts them. You have the moral authority to say, "Don't be afraid" and make it stick.

Wisdom vs. Knowledge

Whenever I can't figure out the latest technology, I try to find a twelve-year-old to tell me what to do. Yes, the world is a bit upside down. Children are teaching adults how to survive in the age of technology. It can make us think we have nothing to teach our grandchildren.

Maybe you don't know how to play the newest video game, and your smartphone makes you look stupid. Yes, your nine-year-old granddaughter can film a video and edit it. She understands technology, even if she can't yet spell the word. She may soon be able to command a robot to make her bed, but she doesn't understand life. You do. You know what love and encouragement can do. You know why you shouldn't lie and why you should make your bed. You have survived a lot. She hasn't even survived her teens.

She lives in a puppy-dog world that chases its tail. Youth are easily drawn to what is new, exciting, eye-catching, and famous. So were we. We too grew up in a world oriented to the secular, to wealth, to fame, and to success. Maybe our movies were not as much about revenge justice, high body counts, explosions, and justifying superficial sex. We saw more movies that emphasized the importance of ordinary self-sacrificing love and forgiving those who did you wrong, but we did chase our tails as well.

Wisdom comes with age, and our "older" values actually can sell well to youth. Proven, tested, lasting, right, and true— these are wisdom-based values. They are attractive. You can offer what the hottest singer and the coolest actor cannot.

Wisdom is the ability to discern what is most important, why it is important, and what it demands in response. There is a big difference between wisdom and technological knowledge. You have an abundance of the first. Better technology can't replace what you have: love, courage, patience, long-suffering, laughing, and crying. You understand these things, the deeper, more meaningful things of life.

Wisdom still works when new and exciting fail. You are no longer a puppy chasing its tail.

Faith

You have a mature faith. That faith is comprised of three distinguishable elements: the worship and experience of God, the content of belief, and living morally. All three can be passed on to your grandchildren.

Faith: The Worship and Experience of God

There are easy and obvious ways to invite your grandchildren into your everyday worship of God, such as giving thanks before and after meals, or bringing them to Mass and explaining the meaning of what is taking place.

The Catholic faith has a strong skeleton, a structure that strengthens the worship behavior of a believer. It provides set prayers, sacraments, and ways of relating to God. But those bones need to live, as Ezekiel would say (see Ezekiel 37:1-14). Children don't have the full capacity for a broad or deep spiritual life that an adult has. Their brains don't finish maturing until they are in their early twenties. As with other things in life, such as saying please and thank you, we teach children right behavior first. The deep understanding of and appreciation for that behavior come later. This is why we teach set prayers to children.

The liturgical life of the Church is important. Children love order, structure, and repetition. My siblings and I complained the year my mother changed the menu for Christmas dinner. We wanted it to stay the same. You know that marvelous age when children say, "Again, let's do it again." Again and again! There is a beauty in order and repetition.

Faith, in many ways, begins with doing what should be done. Saying please and thank you to God is as important as saying it at the dinner table.

Morning and bedtime prayer, prayers before meals, Sunday Mass, and regular Confession—these are the basics that ought to be in place. They are important building blocks for children. Still, the more your grandchildren see that God is part of your everyday life, the better. Your faith is not private. It is not a Sunday-only reality. It is not just scaffolding.

You pass on your experience of God by bringing your grandchildren into your relationship with him. You model it every time you pray spontaneously or talk about God over the course of the day. When your grandchildren visit your home, you can bring them into your Bible reading, ask them what they would like you to pray for on their behalf, and, especially, find an opportunity to talk with them about your own faith journey.

My sister has two grandchildren whose parents aren't actively involved in the Church, but they don't mind that she is passing on her faith to them. Whenever the family is at her house, she makes sure to say grace before meals. They know this is how things are done at Grandma's. She has also begun shuttling the grandchildren, ages ten and twelve, to school. They leave before breakfast to avoid the traffic and stop near the school to have muffins at the Kwik Trip, where they say grace before eating. "Bless us, O Lord . . ."

Then, in one week her grandson broke his elbow, her son hurt his foot at work, and our brother had emergency surgery on his back. So she did more than the simple "Bless us, O Lord" prayer at Kwik Trip; she added a prayer naming those who needed healing: our brother, her son, and her grandson. Before she finished with "In the name of the Father . . . ," her granddaughter interrupted and added, "and God make Grandma's back better so that she can finish sewing my winter jacket as well."

Needless to say, she was pleasantly surprised by her granddaughter's addition, but that's what happens when you invite people into your experience of God. They experience him too. When you pray, they pray. But the experience of God has to move beyond external behavior. It is important for them to experience God and his action internally as well. A child's experience of God needs to be hers and not just hearing about yours.

You can "midwife" a child's faith. You can help him see the invisible God at work. You can help awaken his faith. Even better, you can help him understand what is behind the awe and wonder he already perceives in this world.

All human beings can describe an experience of wonder from their childhood, whether it was the first time they saw an ocean, a mountain, or a waterfall. As St. Paul says in his Letter to the Romans, "Ever since the creation of the world his invisible nature, namely, his eternal power and deity, has been clearly perceived in the things that have been made" (1:20).

We perceive God's invisible nature in the things he has created. He is awesome because he creates awesome things. His infinite and all-powerful nature is reflected in reality. Nature is his mirror. One of the most enjoyable things you can do is help your grandchildren look into that mirror.

When you help your grandchildren connect the dots between wonder and God, the One who causes it, you help them see that "this is that!" It is an "Aha!" moment for them. Wonder and beauty are connected to a person, God, and you just gave your grandchildren the way to make sense of what they have experienced: "I was made to know The-One-Who-Is-Wonderful."

God makes himself known to all children as the unknowable, invisible, almighty, wonderful, and good person he is before they can ever describe or define what unknowable, invisible, almighty, wonderful, and good even mean. That sense of awe is the doorway to faith: "The fear of the LORD is the beginning of wisdom, / and the knowledge of the Holy One is insight" (Proverbs 9:10).

What does that passage mean? If wisdom is understanding the most important things, where does wisdom begin? It begins with the fear of the Lord. Most of us think that the fear of the Lord is best summarized with a statement like "Now I'm really in trouble!" But fear of the Lord is possibly better understood as the upside of fear, that is, awe. "Whoa!" is also a form of fear. It stops us in our tracks. "Wow!" It fills us with wonder. "What is that?" It awakens our curiosity. We want to know. The search for wisdom has begun, and it has begun with the fear of the Lord, with the experience of awe.

A strategic grandparent is ready for such moments. Sometimes they come as a surprise when your grandson sees something new: a frog catching a fly with its tongue. Sometimes you can anticipate it because your granddaughter is about to see the ocean for the first time. A strategic grandparent knows how to respond to a "wow" experience with a grandchild who has just witnessed the wonderful God, the creator of all these amazing things we enjoy. Often you only need to point it out.

You can be one of those who helps awaken faith in your grandchild's life. What a joy it is to see that happen!

Faith Is Also the Content of Belief

You, as grandparents, pass on what you believe. What you believe has been handed on to you from those who taught you: your parents, teachers, priests, nuns, and catechists. It came from many people.

What do you believe?

"I believe . . ." That is how the Apostles' Creed begins. The creed summarizes our faith in succinct form that goes back to the early days of the Church, when it was used both liturgically and to teach the faith to newcomers:

I believe in God,
the Father Almighty,
creator of heaven and earth.

I believe in Jesus Christ,
his only Son, our Lord,

He was conceived by the
power of the Holy Spirit
and born of the Virgin Mary.

He suffered under Pontius Pilate,
was crucified, died and was buried.
He descended into hell.

On the third day he rose again.

He ascended into heaven,
and is seated at the right hand the Father.
He will come again to judge
the living and the dead.

I believe in the Holy Spirit,
the holy catholic Church,
the communion of Saints,
the forgiveness of sins,
the resurrection of the body,
and the life everlasting.
Amen.

The Apostles' Creed gets you started. The next step up is the catechism. It is likely that you used a catechism in your religion classes when you were a child. You might also remember reviewing faith-related topics with your children when they were preparing for the sacraments or taking religion class in school, but you've probably forgotten much of this content.

Most of us haven't ever had our hands on an adult catechism. Some of us bought the *Catechism of the Catholic Church*, but it is a long book, and we might not have finished it. You might find it helpful to have something shorter but still thorough. There are numerous versions available, such as the *Compendium of the Catechism of the Catholic Church*. In Appendix C, I have provided a short outline of the *Catechism* that might serve as a useful reminder.

Your grandchildren will benefit from your knowledge of doctrine and the *Catechism* and thus your knowledge of the content of your faith. When you speak of your faith, they might realize that you have a consistent way of viewing the world that makes sense and answers the big questions of life.

Faith: Living Morally

The third element of our faith is living morally—that is, living right, doing good, and avoiding wrongdoing. It is exactly what St. Paul exhorts the church at Philippi to do:

> Whatever is true, whatever is honorable, whatever is just, whatever is pure, whatever is lovely, whatever is gracious, if there is any excellence, if there is anything worthy of praise, think about these things. (Philippians 4:8)

A Concise Catholic Catechism puts it this way:

> Human beings have an inborn moral sense. We quickly recognize the same moral principles as true. These principles make up natural law. It defines good and evil, truth and falsehood, helping us know what we must and must not do.[1]

Very few parents want children who are stubborn, impatient, unruly, and dishonest. Even the most unbelieving parents will support you in your efforts to help your grandchildren gain the basic virtues. How many of your grandsons could use a little more patience? How many granddaughters could use a little more control over one of their emotions? You probably know already. You were their age once.

There are many virtues to think about: charity, commitment, compassion, contentment, cooperation, courage, empathy, faith, forgiveness, generosity, graciousness, gratitude, honesty, hope, humility, justice, kindness, loyalty, meekness, patience, peace, perseverance, prudence, respect, tact, temperance, and zeal.

A list like that is helpful. It not only identifies virtues to work on but also offers virtues for you to model. One way to help young people grow in virtue is to live out those virtues for them. God has given us Christ himself as a model to imitate. In addition, we have Mary and a huge number of saints to inspire us in sanctity. It's noteworthy that the saints aren't cookie-cutter versions of one human being. The lives of St. Thomas Aquinas and St. Francis of Assisi are quite different, as are those of St. Catherine of Siena and St. Therese, but they all "put on Christ" (Galatians 3:27).

I hope that what it means to pass on your faith to your grandchildren is a bit clearer now: you pass on the experience of God, the doctrine of the Church, and the moral way of life. Passing on your faith doesn't happen in one step, but here is the story of one grandfather who has been working at it for years. It is a story of passing on his faith in all three forms to his teenage grandson:

Our cabin is in the woods up north. It's a family-owned property used by the descendants of me and two of my siblings. It is a nice, cozy log cabin with pine walls and a huge, field-stone fireplace. There is enough room to sleep thirteen people.

Each fall, a subset of all those who use it meet up north and work together to put away the summer stuff and ready the cabin for the winter. The crew this year was eleven: myself, my brother, my nephew and his son, my oldest son and his son (age twenty-seven), my three sons-in-law and two of their sons.

Like many modern families, we have members of a variety of churches, but all who were at the cabin were churchgoers. So we did our own style of "family prayer" there together, which I led. We sang, prayed, and did a Bible study. We read the story of the rich, young ruler in Mark 10:17-31.

Each person read a verse of the story, and all participated in the discussion of it. We discussed whether there was anything in our lives that was coming between us and Jesus and how to handle it.

I suggested that the real issue of the rich young ruler was not his love for his riches but, rather, the poverty of his faith. We then prayed for the needs of each of those present. When we prayed for my grandson, who is in tenth grade at a large public high school, I had a nudge from the Lord. I asked him rhetorically, "What is the most difficult word to say in the English language?"

After a short pause, I answered my own question: "It is the word 'No!,' especially when the temptation is to say 'Yes.'" So, I prayed for my grandson that the Lord would keep him safe from all the temptations of high school and that he especially would have the strength to say "No!"

Four weeks later some of his friends from the cross-country team saw a run-down building with a "no trespassing" sign. They wanted to go and explore. He said, "No, that's not the right thing to do."

The others went anyway, got caught by the police, were sentenced to perform community service, and were disqualified from the cross-country team for the season.

My grandson's "No!" resulted in the lot of us saying "Yes!" because he handled the peer pressure.

This grandfather had faith. He set up an opportunity to pass on the content of his faith through a Bible study. He acted on it by passing on a moral truth to his grandson, and he manifested his own experience of God in prayer.

Special Ingredients

You have six special ingredients that few ordinary youth workers have in the same way that you do:

- You have time to waste on love for years to come.
- You have a different kind of presence and approachability that no other adult has.
- You have a strong identity.
- You are a model of commitment and stability, a stabilizing force in your grandchildren's lives in a rapidly changing and unsettling world.
- You have the wisdom that comes from experience.
- You have faith that is worth passing on to your grandchildren.

As any cook knows, it is easy to make ordinary spaghetti, but it is the special ingredients that make Grandma's better than anyone else's.

Having said that, let's see if we can multiply your impact as a grandparent by nabbing some youth ministry skills.

CHAPTER 3

BECOMING A YOUTH WORKER

Reaching the next generation has always been an important part of the strategy of the Church. In today's world, youth workers and youth programs are important avenues for passing on faith to young people. Youth workers are on the side of young people; they are role models; they understand the world young people live in, and that puts them in a position to pass on their faith.

Developing a better understanding of modern youth is the first step in becoming a youth worker. Things aren't the same as they were when you were young.

Moan No More

"Young people just aren't the same anymore. The world has really changed."

—grandpas and grandmas from every age

The temptation to complain about youth is as old as dirt. We aren't the first to complain about how young people are missing the mark. You may have seen the following quote:

> The world is passing through troublous times. The young people of today think of nothing but themselves. They have no reverence for parents or old age. They are impatient of all restraint. They talk as if they knew everything, and what passes for wisdom with us is foolishness with them. As for the girls, they are forward, immodest and unladylike in speech, behavior and dress.

There are many quotes like this floating around the internet. They are often attributed to a sermon by Peter the Hermit in AD 1274, but Peter the Hermit died in AD 1115. Oops!

Hesiod, Socrates, and Plato each get credited with very similar quotes, but my favorite is this fabricated quote from a six-thousand-year-old Egyptian tomb: "We live in a decaying age. Young people no longer respect their parents. They are rude and impatient. They frequently inhabit taverns and have no self-control." If this quote actually existed, it would be the oldest known instance of writing, appearing a thousand years before any previously discovered instances! Whoever made up that quote wasn't an archeologist.

Bad peers, ineffective parenting, and toxic cultures have produced unruly youth for millennia. Socrates' grandfather probably complained about Socrates' peers and how much had gone bad in just a few years.

That's not to deny that things can change for the worse. If you recently came out of a coma that started in 1999, you would be utterly at sea with today's technology, sexuality, cultural norms, politics, world map, and the words we use to describe it all, such as the following:

A tiger mom checks in on her cisgender and bigender sons, who are hate-watching a YouTube bromance video on separate smartphones. She googles "man date" and sees a meme of some metrosexual (guy, she thinks) who is sexting a girl who has been ghosting him.

Checking in on her tween daughter, who is binge-watching Netflix and surreptitiously vaping a fruit-flavored Juul, the mom notices her daughter swipe left on her iPhone, changing screens to Amazon where she adds some yoga pants to her cart and says, "Bootylicious. I need to get a selfie wearing those and post it on Instagram."

This woke mom thinks to herself, "She and I need to FaceTime more" (since they don't actually talk face-to-face). Mom is worried that her girl might be getting body shamed by at least one of her BFFs.

The tiger mom can't wait for her wife to get home.

Yup, it's a different world.

Top Teen Challenges

Google "top ten challenges teens face," and you will see a pretty consistent set of lists from the National Institute of Mental Health, parents, counselors, youth ministers, and teens themselves. Some of the challenges are new, such as those related to the internet. Some are a twist on long-standing challenges, such as relationship problems or academics. Some are old, such as peer and parent pressure or alcohol and drugs.

These ten challenges appear on most lists:

- Stress and anxiety. Both have risen compared to fifty years ago but are still mainly related to academics, others' expectations, and the struggle teens have in managing their time and their lives.

- Low self-esteem. What is noteworthy here is not low self-esteem itself but its new primary cause—body image—rather than social class, race, intelligence, athletic ability, or poverty.

- Pressure to conform. Teens feel strong pressure to conform, coming from their peers, as well as parents, teachers, and other authorities.

- Drugs, alcohol, smoking, and vaping. Some of the drugs are new. Many of the old ones are now stronger.

- Depression, self-harm, and suicide. All are rising rapidly among youth.

- Internet and screen addiction. This is new. Social media, video games, and pornography are far more addicting than television, and the number of addicted youth is far higher than in the pre-internet era.

- Sexuality and gender. Teen pregnancy and underage sex aren't new (and both have been decreasing recently). Sexually transmitted diseases are rising. Abortion doesn't appear on most lists, but that's another story. Gender dysphoria will almost certainly be on any upcoming list.

- Bullying. This wouldn't have been on the top-ten list fifty years ago.

- Family issues. Divorce, abuse, fighting, and absence of the father or mother are continuing problems.

- Lack of purpose. This can include the human need for a sense of purpose, such as knowing why I am in school, or the spiritual, such as knowing the purpose of my life.

Let's add a few other big issues to fill out the picture.

Too Fast, Too Furious

Your grandchildren live in a fast-paced world. While it is true there are only 168 hours per week for everyone, increased stress comes from trying to do more in the same amount of time. Fast-food, immediate gratification, the overwhelming pace of life, and the opportunities for distraction aren't good. A faster sunset wouldn't make it more beautiful. Wolfing food doesn't make it more nutritious or taste better.

The fast pace of life drives us to squeeze more into shorter amounts of time. Inevitably, this leads to a drop in quality, and young people need quality, especially quality time. Your well-spent hour with them is far better than twenty that are poorly spent. If you want to be a strategic grandparent and successful youth worker, spend quality time with your grandchildren.

Moral Confusion

Young people are confused by the different moral approaches of the people around them. Their parents, teachers, coaches, priest, boss, and friends express different views on abortion, legal marijuana, climate change, social media, pornography, sexual identity issues, and religion. Young people themselves are also facing new issues. Young women are asking if it is OK to sell their eggs to a fertility clinic. Young men on wrestling teams are being shamed for refusing to wrestle girls.

Which way is up, which is down, and does it matter? They know about fake news, but most of it seems fake. They look at internet pictures where everyone has a fake web page with fake smiles, but when they talk to their friends who posted all those smiling faces, they realize that many of them are depressed, aimless, and relationally starved.

What is true, good, and beautiful? Who is trustworthy? They don't know, and it is only becoming harder to know who, if anyone, is telling the truth or whether truth even exists anymore. As youth say, "It's complicated."

Where Do I Fit In?

I grew up in the sixties and seventies. I wore those clothes. I was a nonconformist—just like everyone else in my school. I was "outta sight" and "groovy." I wanted to fit in, and, at the same time, I wanted to stand out. I wanted to be an adult, sometimes, sort of, but not yet.

Youth today also want to fit in. They have all been told that they are special and belong, but that is not their experience. Their world is inclusive in theory but exclusive in fact. Cliques and bullying have not gotten better, but worse. Modern youth are more troubled by the fact that they don't fit in and don't measure up. They are too tall, too short, too fat, too thin, too smart, too dumb. They get plastic surgery to remove a chin dimple because they want to look better, but it doesn't make them feel more confident.

The idea that you can fit in anywhere you want, however you want, and that everyone else will accept you is patently false. They know that. They want it to be true, but it isn't. Indeed, they have worked their way through a dozen "best friends forever," and some are no longer even on speaking terms.

"Will I ever fit in? Where?" That is the fear plaguing many young people.

In Summary

It would be foolish not to identify the negative things about modern youth culture. It would also be foolish to focus too much on them.

Older people tend to see negative things. We can be tempted to moan, "The world has changed, and young people aren't the same anymore," but that does not equip us or anyone else to make a difference. Moaning is mostly a waste of time.

Good youth workers do see the struggles youth face, but they have an amazing ability to focus on the positive things instead. They want the best for the youth they serve. Like them, we need to choose a positive approach. We need a winning mindset. Talking to a coach about why his team lost isn't the best strategy if we're looking for someone to help us win. Talking to a winning coach—that's what we need to do. So . . .

Youth Work 101

Let's look at principles of effective youth work and what successful youth workers can teach us as grandparents who want to be there for our grandchildren and to pass on our faith to them.

Most people can identify the most important elements of youth work:

- high-impact events such as retreats, summer camps, and mission trips;
- the weekly youth program;
- good peer-group dynamics;
- service to others;
- and, especially, youth workers.

Grandparents probably aren't the best candidates to run a weekly youth program, to be their grandchildren's peers, or to run a summer camp. You probably won't read this book and then fill out an application for a job as a youth worker. That isn't the goal. The goal is to help you become a strategic grandparent who has picked up, from youth workers, a few ways to act strategically in the lives of your grandchildren.

Here are ten youth-work principles that every grandparent doing youth work should know. (There are others, but this will get you through Youth Work 101.)

YW 101.1: Lead from Alongside

There are tons of books available about leadership. Many of them will tell you why it is important to lead from the front—like George Washington crossing the Delaware. "Follow me." Others promote leading from the back—getting others up and doing, such as when Jesus sent the disciples out two by two. "You do it!" Still others promote leading from the middle, like a basketball coach in a huddle. "We can still win this!"

Youth work recognizes all these leadership styles as important. Grandparents have to lead from the front at times. At other times they mainly cheer from the bleachers. But much of youth work is built around "us together"—leading from alongside.

I learned to ride a bike in the same way almost everyone else learned—with help. My "coach" demonstrated how to do it, but the goal was for me to learn to do it. When he said, "Just try it," I didn't find that very helpful (leading from behind). Nor was watching him and hearing, "Just do what I am doing" (leading from the front). What helped most was having him beside me, steadying me, giving me a little push, running beside me just in case I tipped. That was the leadership I needed. I learned from someone running alongside me. Eventually, I taught my younger brother and sister how to ride a bike the same way.

Youth work isn't a top-down methodology. It is an alongside methodology that is present, trusted, admired, steadying, courage building, and empowering. It is the fun of "Yes, we can!" and the joy of "You did it!"

Sometimes grandparents are substitute parents. They have times when they must work from the top down, but in the usual course of life, the "alongside" option is their default position.

YW 101.2: Keep a Positive Focus

Bad things have a way of seeping into young people's lives. It might be an overly sexualized way of dressing for a ten-year-old girl or a first exposure to a highly addictive video game for a young boy. That's tough for us to see, especially if the girl is your granddaughter or if the boy is your grandson.

"How do I address that?" we ask. "I probably don't even want to know all the bad things my grandchildren are exposed to. Is there a way to keep those things out? Can we build the perfect wall or defense?"

Unfortunately, the answer is no. There is no perfect defense. Fortunately, in youth work, the focus is on building virtue more than it is on correcting faults. Positive air pressure (virtue) can keep a huge amount of bad stuff out. The best way to help your grandchildren isn't to be the filter of all bad things. It is to be the promoter of some of the best things.

It's not helpful to say, "When I was a boy, I didn't sass my mother, watch anything without permission, or play before I did my chores and homework." A grandfather who thinks like a youth worker knows how useless, or even counterproductive, such a critique can be. Being critical isn't actually what our grandchildren need from us. They need us to help them build virtue, and that is a joy to do.

I grew up in Minnesota and attended baseball games at the Metrodome in Minneapolis. The building itself provides a great example of the power of the positive.

You entered the stadium through revolving doors and didn't notice the high air pressure that was holding up the cloth roof. When the game ended, however, the exit doors opened. As soon as you walked in front of the doors, you were swept outside. The positive pressure blew you right out of the stadium. It blew everything out—and nothing seeped in. Positive internal air pressure kept even mosquitoes out of the stadium.

The Metrodome serves as a good model for how to keep bad stuff out of young people's lives. Fill their hearts, their minds, and their time with good things. Make it hard for the bad to seep in.

You know what the good things are. You know how to do them. Most grandchildren will happily play upbuilding games or listen to Grandma read a great Bible story. These build in the positive air pressure. Children learn virtue if we teach it. Fill a child's time with good things, and goodness results. Repeated practice instills positive behavior that eventually becomes a virtue.

The Boy Scouts are an example of the power of a positive focus. A scout is to be "trustworthy, loyal, helpful, friendly, courteous, kind, obedient, cheerful, thrifty, brave, clean, and reverent." When I first encountered the Boy Scout Law, that list of virtues seemed right and true.

Paul's Letter to the Galatians gives us another list of virtues: "love, joy, peace, patience, kindness, goodness, faithfulness, gentleness, [and] self-control" (Galatians 5:22-23).

Building positive attitudes and habits into your grandchildren can be done either passively or actively. Passive character building is simply modeling the basic human virtues in our day-to-day lives for our grandchildren to imitate. The grandpa who hits his thumb with a hammer will model either wrong speech or self-control. When he models self-control, it is an example that a young boy will likely find inspiring. It is an example of passive virtue building because it depends on his grandson seeing and choosing to imitate his grandfather.

Active character building is strategic. You have to think about how you can instill virtue into your grandchildren. Many of the stories that are submitted to our website are from strategic grandparents actively working to instill virtue in their grandchildren.

This story, sent in by Tim Shireman, tells how he helped his grandson with overcoming grumpiness:

At the age of sixty-nine, I have fallen victim to the "Grumpy Grandpa Syndrome." I find myself complaining about many things: my various aches and pains, not being able to do things I used to do, or about the state of the world in general.

I've noticed one of my grandsons has fallen into this pattern as well. He complains about a variety of things: having to do his homework, not being allowed to watch as much TV as he would like, having limits on the time he spends playing video games, etc. I certainly don't want him to be a "Grumpy Grandson."

The Episcopal church I attend does not corporately observe Lent. Almost everyone, though, has some concept of this religious period of prayer and fasting. At the very least, most of us have heard this question: "What are you giving up for Lent?" Some people know the Bible basis for Lent that says we should fast, pray, and give alms.

Lent can be about more than just self-denial. It can be a time to focus on growing in virtue. I find that my self-improvement strategies tend to fall short unless I team up with someone else for added support. That got this strategic grandfather thinking about making a difference in my grandson's life. I decided to team up with him!

So I set up a "Put a Smile on It" competition with my grandson this Lent. Together we made a Lenten calendar poster to track how we did each day with either a smiley or grumpy face. Whenever we got together, we would share our progress and the strategies we were using to overcome our respective "grumpies."

At the end of Lent, we counted who had the most smiley faces on the poster. (Next Lent, I think we will work on honesty!)

I didn't say whether the winner or loser would buy lunch afterward, but I bought lunch and we talked about how we have improved in being joyful. Honestly, I think it helped me regardless of whether it helped him. In the end, I think we both won. Wait, our near circle of friends probably won too!

The easy thing about educating children in virtue is that they usually signal what they lack. An observant grandparent can see when it is time to help them gain self-control, kindness, thankfulness, or courage.

YW 101.3: Safe Spaces

A grandmother of three and former youth minister says,

Once a youth minister, always a youth minister. I am repeatedly making use of my youth ministry skills as I work with my grandchildren. There is a huge overlap in the skill sets necessary for grandparenting and youth work. I'm enjoying my "second round" in youth ministry, but I use a lot of what we taught in Youth Work 101.

As a youth minister, I got into a place of trust in the lives of teens. How? We spent time together, got to know one another, and this built trust. As a grandmother, I have done the same, but every once in a while, that trust gets tested. Teens especially know how to test the waters of trust. They will throw out a comment and see what response comes. If the response is too hot and the preaching or correcting starts, their ears shut down and they may never raise a trust issue again. If the response is too cold and you pass off what they are saying as trivial, the discussion stops. You didn't hear their measured call for help.

Sometimes the right response is a patient one. Just like you can't eat a whole chicken in one bite, some conversations can't be finished in one sitting.

My older granddaughter was about eleven, and we were driving in the car when she asked out of the blue, "Grandma, how do you know if you might be lesbian?" My first thought was, "I didn't even know what that word meant when I was your age, and if I had, I sure wouldn't have asked my grandmother about it!"

Instead, I responded, "Oh . . . What makes you think that you might be lesbian?"

She replied, "I just don't like boys."

"So," I said, "what don't you like about them?"

"They make me so mad."

I didn't say, "Honey, wait 'til you get married!" I simply answered, "Well, I'm not sure that makes you lesbian, but we can talk more about it if you want."

She let it drop. So I did as well.

(I did raise it confidentially with my daughter, her mom. I let her know how I handled it, and she encouraged me to continue.) The next time we were in the car, I asked her if she still thought she was lesbian.

She said, "No, Grandma . . . There is this boy . . . and he doesn't make me mad."

I smiled. Not rushing in to "fix her problem" was the best response. Youth of all ages sometimes just need someone who isn't in a rush.

But the key lesson in this story was safety. I doubt my grand-daughter would have ever raised the issue if we weren't in the car. Because I was driving, she knew we wouldn't have eye contact on this, and that made the car a safe place. My youth-work experience taught me the value of emotional safety. I knew better than to raise the issue again anywhere else than in the car. The car was already designated by her as a safe place to talk to Grandma.

What are some other safe spaces besides a car?

- Walking is a side-by-side activity.
- Evening often feels safer than daytime.
- Dimly lit spaces are safer than brightly lit ones.
- Quiet is better than noisy.
- An uninterrupted environment is better than an active environment.

YW 101.4: Listening

The same grandmother also wrote this story on the value of listening:

My grandson was eight years old when his parents divorced. Due to my son's work, I regularly had his two kids stay with me on Sunday nights because I would drive them to school on Mondays and hand them back to their mother. When they would spend the night, I would read with them the Bedtime Blessings *book by Marianne Richmond.*

One night my grandson said, "Will you stay with me, Grandma, until I fall asleep?" This was my cue to listen. He then talked about the difficulties he was having in his new situation with his mother. (He "inherited" four big kids and their dad in the house.)

We talked a bit, and I said that when I get stressed, I pray. He said he didn't know how to pray. So I wrote this prayer for him to say when he got stressed about living in two places and being without his dad to talk to at times.

Dear Leo,

I love you very much and pray for you every day. Here is a prayer for you to say when you get sad and stressed.

Love, Grandma C.

Dear Jesus,

I know that I am made of the best parts of my dad and mom and that they both love me. Jesus, calm me down, and help

*me take a big breath. I know that you are holding me and lov-
ing me when my dad can't be there. I know that my sadness
will soon get better. Amen.*

Love, Leo

He liked that.

*So I asked him, "Do you want to take this with you to your
mom's place?" He said, "No, Grandma; the other kids in the
house might make fun of me. But I know it's here, Grandma."*

*He only wanted someone to listen, but listening opened
another door, a door to prayer.*

YW 101.5: Confidentiality

Her look gave her away. Grandma's seventeen-year-old granddaughter wanted to talk about something.

. . . But she wasn't sure she was ready to tell Grandma.

. . . She was afraid it could have unforeseen consequences.

But she did. "Grandma, I want to tell you something. Promise me that you won't tell my parents, will you?"

"How am I supposed to respond to that?" Grandma thought.

Confidentiality is one of the trickiest parts of doing youth
work. Your granddaughter has come to you and with these
words has put you in a bind. One the one hand, you shouldn't
make an unconditional promise; on the other hand, this young
person is in need of help.

Sometimes a teen wants you to keep something secret because it seems really big to her, but it's actually quite small: "Grandma, I think that boy is cute." She just wants to talk about it so she can gain confidence.

But at other times, the matter might be serious: "Grandma, a friend brought drugs to a sleepover, and we tried them . . ." There is a lot to talk about here. The problem isn't only that your granddaughter tried the drugs but also whom she is hanging out with and the fact that others are also being put at risk.

The "cute boy secret" is worth a smile from you and a few words of understanding: "I remember my first crush . . . ," but the drugs issue is serious.

If a grandma has built a relationship of trust with her granddaughter over the years, she may come to her with some of those risky questions—often with a rider, the assurance that what she says will go no further. She is looking for someone she can trust, someone who is not her mom or dad. She may think she already knows what Mom and Dad would say, but she is still unsettled.

Teens will solicit a promise not to tell for many reasons. They may want to share a private burden or thrill. They may come to you because they know their friends will blab. They may want help dealing with shame, guilt, or confusion, and they may realize they can't handle the situation on their own. They may have a friend in crisis or be experiencing pressure regarding some high-risk behavior.

This much is clear: they are asking for your help, but they are also testing you. Are you more loyal to them or their parents?

So let's go back to the story: "Grandma, I want to tell you something. Promise me that you won't tell my parents, will you?" What do you say? "Of course, sweetheart! I promise." Many would, but it's not the best answer. You don't have enough information about what's coming next.

Let's back up further and ask, "What is really going on here?" Can you see that she has a significant amount of trust in you already? She has already communicated, "This is important to me and delicate. It's risky even to talk about it, but I am taking the first big step in saying I have a delicate issue." She didn't say that, but it is what she is feeling. First, respond to that trust! She needs love first. You don't have to rush to a solution. She is probably afraid, uncertain, angry, sad, or confused and is looking for emotional support more than the "right" answer. Sometimes she needs courage, reassurance, or confidence more than your advice.

Understanding the real situation, what isn't said but is communicated, is being people smart. Understanding the emotional element that drives a teen's need is a key skill in youth work and grandparenting.

Next time a grandchild asks, "Promise you won't tell anyone?" your answer should be people smart. Instead of saying, "I promise," say something like, "You know I'm here for you. Let's talk about it together and see if we can come up with a good solution." You will give her the reassurance she is looking for. You will be addressing her real need, and isn't that what you really wanted to do anyway? You are already in position. She came to you and asked for support because she thinks you can give it. You can. You can offer to walk alongside her. In the end, she may work it out for herself, and you may only have to get behind her: "That's a great idea! Try that!"

Now what if she tells you something her parents really should know? You can help her find the right approach. It probably doesn't start with saying, "You did what!!!?" She probably already regrets what she did. She is looking for help, not the correct opinion and certainly not condemnation!

Once again, the right starting point is alongside her. She came to you, not Mom and Dad, nor her friends. There is probably a reason why, and it is likely that she is looking for someone she trusts emotionally and someone who can offer wisdom.

"Are you afraid of how people (your mom and dad) are going to respond?"

"Yes. Mom and Dad will lose it!"

"Maybe. How?"

"They'll yell and ground me for the rest of my life."

"Do you deserve to be grounded?"

"Well, probably, but not forever!"

"How about if you start with what you just told me. 'Mom and Dad, I'm afraid. I did something that I'm going to be grounded for, and it will probably make you mad. I'm sorry.' How would they respond to that?"

Your discussion will lead somewhere, hopefully to a place where she knows the right thing to do and has the courage to do it. Maybe it won't, but you might be in a position to offer to do something else for her or with her. You might not be able to fix what's wrong, but you also might prevent some potential bad results.

You may have to say, "Sweetie, there is an important moral issue here for both of us. I think you understand that you have to talk to your parents about this and that I can't just let it slide." You may need to take a strong stand, but you can't teach integrity if you don't practice it.

No matter what the outcome, go home and pray, whether it's "Thanks!" or "Help!"

YW 101.6: Service to Others

Children have a preference for play over responsibility. As they mature, they start to enjoy having responsibility. First, they play "mom and dad." Later, they begin to find a reward in serving. Serving others is a form of love and because God made us for love, human beings sense fulfillment by loving. "I am at my best when I love."

Most youth groups find that mission trips to serve the poor have a big impact on youth. They see others in real need, and they see the difference they can make by digging a well or building a house. They also grow in thankfulness for what they have.

Giving your grandchildren real responsibilities makes a long-term difference. Studies show that one of the strongest correlations with adult happiness is having done childhood chores.

Norma Wittgens tells this story that illustrates the value of simple homegrown service. Most of the service we all do in our lifetime is, in fact, local. It is for those we see most every day.

Several years ago, my husband and I moved to be nearer our family. Many of our grandchildren now live within one mile of our home, which is on the Grand River. We envisioned family outings for fishing, canoeing, kayaking, picnics, bonfires, and maybe even some swimming, but there was one obstacle: a ten-foot drop from our yard down to the riverbank.

We commissioned our son-in-law, Christopher, to design an answer. He did. It would take twenty-three steps and ten yards of gravel. He built the forms, but we needed some "boy power." We asked our older grandsons, ages eight through twelve, to help transport the gravel down to the steps for Uncle Chris. We also asked them to invite their friends to help.

On the day of the project, ten boys showed up to work. Grandpa led them in a prayer for safety on the job, courtesy and kindness among the boys, teamwork, a good work attitude, and fun for the boys and the satisfaction that they had each done his best. Duties were assigned, and the boys were encouraged to engage in positive speech while working. For two and a half hours, they encouraged and helped each other. Grandpa and Grandma doled out many compliments on their efforts.

When the job was complete, Grandpa paid our "men" five dollars each. The boys congratulated each other and exchanged high fives. Mission accomplished. Grandpa finished the project with prayer, thanking the Lord for each of the boys; their talents; freedom from injury; the building of good relationships; a job well-done; and, of course, for the food, because it was now time for a pizza party and root beer floats.

Today, everyone can get to the river safely and without difficulty. Those steps are a blessing for us! But they were also a blessing for the boys. I don't mean the physical steps. The boys took character steps: hard work, cooperation, patience, faith...

Yes, we all benefit from having access to the river, but the real gain was learning the joy of doing service for others.

Service is a step toward responsible adulthood. Serving together with your grandchildren is a double win. They take steps toward adulthood, and you deepen your relationship with them.

Here are sixteen ideas for how to serve together with your grandchildren:

1. Send cards to soldiers serving overseas.
2. Deliver Meals on Wheels with your grandchild's help.
3. Tutor children together.
4. Coach a youth sports team together.
5. Put on a comedy or music performance for the elderly.
6. Organize an Easter egg hunt for neighborhood children.
7. Make birthday cards for the elderly with no family.
8. Organize Christmas caroling together with others.
9. Sponsor an animal at your local zoo.
10. Volunteer at a soup kitchen.
11. Adopt a local highway, and clean up trash along it.
12. Organize a service team of seniors and teens together to do any of the above, and host a celebration afterward.

13. Collect blankets to give to a homeless shelter.

14. Collect unused makeup and perfume to donate to a women's center.

15. Collect baby clothes and supplies to donate to new parents.

16. Collect used sports equipment to donate to those who need it.

YW 101.7: Conversation Skills

When I first started to do youth work, I didn't know that the hardest part would be mastering the art of conversation with tweens and teens. I learned that quickly, though.

As I reached my late twenties, I had to do much more work to stay up-to-date on current topics and slang. Young people no longer spoke my language. I was in danger of becoming a wet rag if I said wet rag! The real problem, I realized later, is that most young people are not familiar with how to have a good conversation. You need to ask them a lot of questions before they ask you one, and you need to do it in a way that doesn't seem like a nonstop interrogation.

Mastering the art of conversation is one of the most important skills in youth ministry. Youth workers have to do that with new kids over and over. It's easier for grandparents because they have an in with their grandchildren. They don't need to do relationship building with a total stranger.

Alas, mastering the art of conversation is complex because the art differs greatly among children, tweens, teens, and young adults and all the different personality types. I have always found boys between the ages of eleven and thirteen to be the most challenging. When I was in that age group, I found it challenging to talk to anyone, and when I became a youth worker, I still could not penetrate the tween "boy fog." I'd ask a thirteen-year-old boy, "Hi, how are you doing?" He would answer: "Fine." And that was generally followed by an uncomfortable silence.

The trick to maintaining a conversation is being equipped with a bunch of good questions for young people of every age—questions that cannot be answered with the words: fine, good, OK, nothing, yes, or no. Then you need to have a way to continue the conversation thereafter. Even so, getting good at it takes work.

Here are a few questions for elementary-aged children:

- What was the best part of your day? (Yes, they can answer lunch, but are you ready with a follow-up?) "Lunch. Must have been an amazing lunch or a really bad day. Which one?"
- What's the biggest difference between this year and last year in school?
- What is your favorite class? What do you like most about it? What is your least favorite class? Why?
- If you had a whole day to do anything you wish, what three things would you do?
- Did I ever tell you about . . . (and have a good story to tell).
- A fun competition: Who can hold their breath longer, you or me? Who can count to ten the fastest?

Here are a few for tweens:

- If you opened a store, what would you sell?
- What can you do that you could teach to someone else?
- Tell me about what you read for history class.
- What is the easiest subject you have in school?
- What rules at school are different from the rules at home? Do you think they're fair?
- What do you and your best friend like to do together?

Here are a few for teenagers:

- What is the worst junk food on the planet?
- Which was worse: elementary school or middle school? Why?
- Who is your favorite teacher and why?
- If there were going to be one rule that everyone on earth would have to follow, what would it be?
- What do you want to have as your first paid job?
- If you could be a teacher, a restaurant owner, or a politician, which would you be and why?

If you say of at least one of those questions, "I would never ask my grandchild that!" then you probably have the ability to make up better questions!

Ultimately, youth workers know that kids will talk about themselves, their needs, and their interests. Part of the joy of working with youth is discovering the topics they want to discuss. As a grandparent, you can do what no youth worker can: you can tell them you want to help them learn how to have a good conversation and to master the give-and-take of conversation with adults. You will know you have made progress when they ask you a question without prompting. You can help them grow in self-confidence, but their confidence in you will also grow. You will be creating trust, and then, when those magic conversations happen, you will be glad you did what you did.

Let me add one more thing about good conversations here. A good youth worker knows when to stop talking. If you "over-talk" someone's interest capacity, you will lose on two counts. The good things you said won't stick, and you will have wasted some precious relational capital.

YW 101.8: Going Deep

Good youth workers know that their most significant work is done one-on-one. How does that translate to grandparent-ing? The time to start doing one-on-one work is now. The deep conversation that happens when a grandson or granddaughter is fifteen will be set up by doing things one-on-one over the ten previous years.

I know several grandfathers who have made it a point to have one-on-one time with their grandsons by the time they hit first grade. A one-on-one experience won't last long at that age, but the grandfathers are setting up a pattern of quality time that will turn from carbon into diamond.

With boys, it generally means doing something first, because "doing together" allows for talking about something "out there," something not personal, something objective, like the importance of truth in friendship. If time with grandpa regularly includes into-the-deep questions, especially ones that go both ways—grandpa to grandson and grandson to grandpa—the one-on-one times will get deeper as the boy grows up. In fact, those conversations will be likely to begin to happen spontaneously.

Nanna, a grandmother from New York, told this story that took her conversations deeper:

The question bag is an idea that came from praying about my grandchildren. (I have eighteen of them, ranging in age from three months to nineteen years, with an assortment of personalities and interests.) One day while praying for them, I asked the Holy Spirit what I could do to love them and share my faith; I knew the answer as soon as I heard it. "Spend TIME with each of them individually."

In response to the Holy Spirit's prompting, I came up with the idea of the question bag! It made asking questions "mysterious" and more fun. I searched the internet for questions pertinent to children ages five to eleven and twelve to fifteen. I copied the questions I thought were appropriate and put them in two labeled bags. Some questions were simple: "What's your favorite birthday dinner? What's your most fun family activity?" Some were deeper and more thought provoking: "What do you think heaven will be like? What does it mean to be a good friend? If you could go back three years in time, what advice would you have given your previous self?"

I took the older ones out for breakfast or ice cream. With the younger ones, I visited the pet store or a park. Typically, over food or snacks, we shared the question bag. I assured them that anything they said would be considered confidential. I allowed them to put back any question they didn't want to answer and draw another. There were no right or wrong answers, but often, additional questions were generated from our discussions. Some grandchildren wanted to answer only a few questions, while others wanted to go through the whole bag!

Over time, the question bag has borne much fruit. I have learned things from my grandchildren, and I have learned things about my grandchildren. I have been able to encourage them regarding situations specific to their own lives. The time spent together has deepened our love for each other.

My grandchildren often mention the question bag, and some will now turn the tables and ask me questions. Last October, I received a phone call from my grandson asking if he could take me out for my birthday lunch. We laughed about the question bag, but both of us knew we could talk more openly and deeply because of that simple, yet powerful, game.

What Nanna did was strategic. She set up a way to go deeper that she felt comfortable using and knew how to use, and she used it. There are lots of ways to set up such opportunities. Take your grandson fishing. Afterward, stop at a Dairy Queen and get an ice cream cone and sit in the park. You have a happy boy who would probably listen to you tell a story about your own conversion or a time when you had to make a tough decision. If you end the story right, you can ask him what he thinks, or "What do you think was the hardest part about that decision?"

Going deep is almost always a function of setting up the right environment, although sometimes it happens serendipitously. It is always the result of putting in the time and building trust before it was ever necessary.

YW 101.9: Group Identity Building

Grandparents don't typically run youth groups—at least, not ordinary weekly ones—but there is something to be said for the periodic "youth event."

Much of the time grandparents spend with their grandchildren is family time, the dynamic of which is spontaneous. One moment you are helping Lili pick colors for her artwork, and not long after, you are hearing from your grandson about his home run in Little League. Such a lively, ever-changing setting, however, makes it hard to pass on your faith in a strategic manner.

Still, it can be done by adding a few touches to special occasions. Thanksgiving dinner (or whatever holiday you host) can include prayer or simply saying what each person is thankful for. Birthdays can be enhanced by saying a few words in honor of the birthday girl after the traditional song is sung and she blows out the candles. The first time you add something like that, it may feel a little forced. If you do it right, however, it will become a good group habit.

So what about organizing a family youth-group time? If you have five grandchildren in a similar age range, you can work with them as a group the way a youth worker would. Let me share two examples with you:

There was an old woman who lived in a shoe.
She had so many children, she didn't know what to do.
Then she had grandchildren, lots of them, too!
"Now . . . Oh now, what will I do?"

Grandma Mini has twenty-seven grandchildren, all of whom live within twenty minutes of her, and sixteen of them are young girls. That's a youth group! She says,

I do granddaughter overnights!

I hosted my first one eight years ago for the six who were eligible, that is to say, potty trained. I'm preparing to host the next one in a couple of weeks for eleven (or maybe twelve by then).

My format is simple. For dinner, it is macaroni and cheese with applesauce or vegetables and a simple dessert.

Next comes a project or activity of some kind. One time it was a tea party, and each granddaughter took home a teacup and saucer. (My collection is embarrassingly large.) Another time we made videos and put them to music. Last time, we made candles. This time we are decorating composition notebooks!

Then we get into our pajamas and watch a movie—usually geared to the youngest granddaughter present. We stop half-way through for popcorn and then finish the movie. Finally, it's off to bed.

In the morning, I make pancakes: plain, blueberry, or choco-late chip. At 11 a.m., they go home.

Why do I do this? One reason is to create memories. Great memories anchor identity. Another reason is to give these wonderful daughters of God a unique chance to interact with one another, to be part of an extended family of faith. A third reason is to learn about exercising the virtues, chiefly the virtue of charity. The older girls help the younger ones with-out even realizing they're doing it, for instance, watching a "little kid" movie with younger cousins or siblings on their laps. They all camp out on the floor in various rooms of the house, and older girls take younger ones into their care: "If you need to go to the bathroom in the middle of the night, wake me up and I'll take you."

Now that the flow of charity is there, I don't have to make it happen. The older girls do it themselves. I might have to facil-itate it once in a while, but mainly I'm a delighted observer.

I love these times, and I hope my granddaughters remember them long after I'm gone.

Another example comes from Rene, a retired nurse and a grandmother. She says,

During my nursing career, well before I was a grandmother, I heard something from one of my patients that stuck with me. Sheryl told me about Cousins Camp. It was a thing she and her husband ran each summer. They lived on a lake, and one week every summer all their older grandchildren (who lived in different states) came to their cabin for Cousins Camp. The week was spent playing in the lake, doing chores, crafts, Bible studies, campfires, and songfests. The grandkids enjoyed Cousins Camp so much that they came back even when they became teenagers.

Cousins Camp became a family tradition. The cousins built strong relationships with one another and their grandparents. They learned life skills, had fun, and grew in their relationship with the Lord.

When I met Sheryl, my children were teenagers. Although grandparenting seemed far away, providing Cousins Camp for my grandchildren became my dream.

Today my husband and I are blessed with four grandchildren, but they live far away. Thanks to Skype, we "see" our Arizona grandkids weekly. I drive 180 miles round-trip every week to spend time with the other grandchildren. We'd like everyone to live closer to us, but we are working with things as they are.

And this year my dream is becoming a reality. My husband and I are beginning Cousins Camp. I am flying to Arizona in June and bringing our six-year-old grandson home for a week. Our three-year-old granddaughter will join us for three days.

All the details aren't worked out yet, but there will be fun, chores, Bible studies, songs, and crafts.

We are beginning small in this new adventure with only two cousins for three days, but it won't be long before the others are able to join us. I am full of hope for the future, hope that love grows within our grandchildren for the Lord and each other. And maybe one day, our grandchildren will have Cousins Camp for their grandkids. I am living one dream and nursing another!

Both of these grandmothers figured out a way to make a group setting work to build faith through an environment they have structured.

YW 101.10: Storytelling

"Did you hear the joke about the grandpa walking back from church with his granddaughter?"

My father was a storyteller and a joke teller. He had an amazing facility to have the right story or joke for any occasion. At my parent's fortieth wedding anniversary celebration, the grandchildren got to say something nice about Grandma Jackie and Grandpa G.T.

They identified all the things you would expect—hugs, smiles, ice cream, listening, presents, candy—and then the youngest, who was seven at the time, got up. She was "a little stinker"—which in our family meant precocious—and said, "What I like about Grandpa G.T. is his stories and his jokes. He always makes me laugh. What I like about Grandma Jackie is that she is a saint, because she listens to the same jokes over and over and over again."

In youth work, storytelling is important. Young people's attention spans aren't that long, but they will listen to stories. Children's books are a three-billion-dollar-per-year business for a reason! Most grandparents already know the value of reading a book to a grandchild, but you may not have thought of doing it this way:

Granny Annie lives in St. Paul, Minnesota, but one of her grandchildren lives a thousand miles away. The idyllic image of a grandchild snuggled up to Grandma as she reads a book happens only once per year, but with today's technology, Granny Annie has found a new way to enjoy reading together.

While visiting her granddaughter, Josie, on the East Coast, she noticed that reading a good book only once was never enough. "Granny Annie, read it again!" Josie would exclaim. She did, over and over, but eventually the time came for her to leave. As soon as she got home, she recorded herself on video reading that same book and sent the recording to her granddaughter. Josie was fascinated. Her mom was also far more pleased to have Josie watch Granny Annie than anything else.

Annie then joined a book-a-month club for children. Now, she chooses a book and has her husband record her reading it. She then sends both the book and the video to her granddaughter, who reads it over and over.

Her husband, Gramps, is more improvisational. He makes up his own stories using toys as props. Small stuffed mom and dad dolls became a big hit, so Josie now has her own mom and dad dolls and retells Gramps' stories or makes up her own and entertains the whole family, whether live or on video.

All Granny and Gramps needed was a smartphone. Initially, they just used the simple video record function. Then they got more creative and are now using multiple cameras and easy-to-use video-editing software. The final project is uploaded in seconds to Google Photos, Google Docs, iMovie, or iCloud and downloaded by her daughter for Josie to watch on her tablet.

So did you hear the joke about the grandpa walking back from church with his granddaughter?

"Did God make you, Opa?" the girl asks.

"Yep! He certainly did," her grandfather answered.

"And then he made me too?" she asks next.

"Of course he did," he answers again.

She nodded her head reflectively and said, "Well, I think he is getting better at it."

Congratulations! You have completed a crash course in Youth Ministry 101. As with everything you learn from a book, it is of value only when you put it into practice.

Do something with at least one of these youth-work skills and see what happens.

CHAPTER 4

THE STRATEGIC GRANDPARENT

There is a difference between being an intentional grandparent and a strategic grandparent. *Intentional* means "done on purpose" or "deliberate." It means you have a motive to get you started or even an outcome in mind. But this book is titled *The Strategic Grandparent.* What is the difference? Being strategic means having a plan, a way to get something done. Passing on your faith to your grandchildren is an excellent intention, a great goal, but it isn't a strategy.

Desiring, wanting, wishing, and intending aren't doing. Thinking, praying, and acting are. The strategic grandparent thinks, prays, and acts strategically.

David: An Example of Thinking, Praying, and Acting Strategically

Ask anyone, "What first comes to mind in association with the biblical character David?" Most will respond with Goliath. A few might identify his adultery with Bathsheba. Some might note his long and glorious reign as the king of Israel, and others, that he wrote seventy-five psalms.

What about David, the strategic grandparent?

David lived to be over seventy years old. He was the father of at least twenty children. Exactly how many grandchildren he had isn't recorded, but we know there were many. Let's look at one particular description of David in his later years.

In Psalm 71 he wrote, "So even to old age and gray hairs, / O God, do not forsake me, / till I proclaim thy might / to all the generations to come" (71:18). When David wrote this psalm, he was almost certainly a grandfather. In it, he reflects on his adversaries, who are saying, "God has abandoned the old man." Considering his troubles at the time, that wasn't unthinkable.

He knew he had limited time left, and he was thinking about how he wanted to use it. Earlier in life, he was thinking about how to conquer more lands. Now he is thinking about how to pass on his faith. How do I use my remaining time? That is thinking strategically.

But the psalm is also a prayer addressed to God. David isn't only thinking strategically, but he is praying strategically; that is, he is asking God for something specific, not just praising or thanking him for what he has done. What does David ask? He wants to tell one more generation, his grandchildren, about God's action in his life.

Further, he isn't only thinking and praying strategically; he is acting strategically. He is writing a song that he (and others) will sing. In the Bible, we read that David had a soothing voice: as a young man, he sang for Saul to calm the king's troubled soul. Even in this psalm, he says he is still singing, gladly and with full voice: "My mouth is filled with thy praise!" (Psalm 71:8) and "My lips will shout for joy" (71:23). It is almost certain he sang to his children and grandchildren about what God had done in his life.

This story about David is a great example of passing on faith—the experience of God, the content of faith, and the moral life all at once—but it is just one example of a grandfather who is always ready to think, pray, and act strategically in passing on his faith.

King David is a great example of a strategic grandparent. What would happen if grandparents began to think, pray, and act strategically like David?

It is time to dive more deeply into how to become a strategic grandparent.

Think Strategically

Thinking Ahead

Thinking strategically begins with anticipating the future and thinking ahead about it.

When I was a child and my grandmother lived with us for a couple of months, I didn't ever think, "OK, I better pay attention to this grandparenting thing because someday I will need to do it!" I wasn't inside my grandma's head, thinking, "Why is she doing this?" I wasn't trying to form a strategy that I might need in fifty years and writing it down in a notebook. I was trying to decide whether a grizzly bear would look OK if I colored it yellow, not dark brown.

Even as a teenager, I barely understood that Grandpa was once young like me. I certainly didn't think, "Someday I will be like my grandfather. I should ask him about what it is like to be seventy and retiring." I didn't ask, "Grandma, what do you think it would be helpful for me to know about grandparenting now so I will able to do it well in forty years?" Or "How do you see your role as a grandmother, especially when it comes to passing on your faith?"

You probably got your second look at grandparenting when you became a parent but quite naturally saw it from a parent's perspective. You were thankful for the love your parents showed to your children. They helped with babysitting, Christmas presents, and a variety of other things. You appreciated their wisdom, love, and encouragement—whether given in words, time, or money. And if they were allies in raising your children, that felt like having an extra set of legs and hands.

Still, as a parent you probably didn't jump ahead to 2020 and think, "I will probably be a grandparent then. I wonder what I can learn now about the role?" You had way too much to figure out about parenting to bother thinking about grandparenting.

Then grandparenting began. It's easy. You have done these things, so you can say, "Grandparenting, I am on top of this!"

My point is that few people think about grandparenting before they begin doing it. Once they begin, not that many think ahead about the role they could play in the future. But when you next pick up your one-year-old granddaughter, look ahead. In a few years, she will hit the curiosity stage. She will be asking you, "Why do I have two eyes if I only see one thing?" "Why don't cats bark like dogs?"

"Why, why, why!"

You know that time will come; you have seen it before. It's an amazing stage of life. "Why" questions are the beginning of the development of reason. Children are starting to understand cause and effect. "Why are clouds white? Why is the grass green? Why do people die? Why do I have to eat vegetables?" Eventually every parent asks, "Why do you have to ask so many questions?"

For a grandparent who wants to pass on faith, "why" questions are a great open door. Many questions a four-year-old asks are based in wonder and awe. As noted before, they are the beginning of a child's search for wisdom.

When a young girl asks why, she has an attentive mind, a mind that can be taught. Thinking ahead means being ready to answer the "why" questions when they come up. When your grandson asks, "Grandpa, why is the sky blue?" a youth worker's instinct is to get right beside that young mind in dialogue. A child isn't looking for the answer a natural science teacher will give him in ninth grade. He is saying, "Wow!" and asking, "Why?"

Get beside him and help him gain knowledge of the Holy One. "Jimmy, isn't blue a cool color? What if God had made the sky purple? We sure wouldn't be as happy as we are, would we? But God loves us; that's why the sky is blue." The physics lesson can wait. He is asking a faith question. Give him a faith answer!

The next time a four-year-old grandson asks, "How old is God?" don't miss your chance! Soon thereafter, your ten-year-old granddaughter will be asking about love. "What is it? Is it more than kissing?" This is a hit-the-jackpot question. You have been given a wide-open door.

Love is more than kissing. It is caring about others more than you care about yourself. It is why Jesus died for us. You might point to a crucifix and say, "That's a reminder that 'God so loved me!'" Love is the basis of our moral code. She may not be able to define "moral code," but she can probably understand that she was made to love and for love. The great commandments are about love, and God gave us those commandments because everything, including ourselves, works better when we love others than when we don't.

Understanding this will have a huge impact on her in years to come. Confidence that she can love and is loved is really important during the "bullying" years of late elementary and junior high school. When youth know they are loved and are encouraged to show love, they are far more resilient against rejection, depression, jealousy, self-hatred, and a host of other problems. Understanding the true nature of love is hugely important for making good decisions about love and sex.

Before you know it, your grandchildren will be in their teens and individuating, that is, deciding for themselves what they believe. They will question, "Do I believe what my parents, teachers, and pastors have taught me about God?" Normally, this isn't a sign of malice or anger. It is the natural process of trying to decide what they will own as their beliefs. Deeper questions about life come up: "Why am I here? What is my purpose in life? What do I believe in?" Typically, they won't have all these questions thought through very well, but they are looking for answers.

During the previous years, you have built up trust. You have given them sound answers. You patiently listened to their questions. You have modeled honesty, goodness, and right speech. You invested pennies earlier, and now you might begin reaping dollars.

You can be among the first adults to ask a teenager's opinion about serious topics. In doing so, you are treating him or her as an adult. Yes, that is risky! You may find yourself in an awkward conversation, but it's great that you are in it. You don't win if you don't play.

What if the opinion your grandson gives isn't the one you hoped to hear? Most adults will simply respond with shut-down correction, but a grandparent can use a youth worker's strategy. You have created room for dialogue by asking him an adult question, and now you need to help him rethink his answer. You might respond, "Thanks for that answer. Let me ask you something." (Start by asking permission to ask.) "You probably know I wouldn't see it quite that way. How do you think I would see it and why?" You have now upped the adult stakes and brought him to a new maturity merely by inviting him to think more deeply. Your response shows that you respect him and his ability to think. By asking him to look again, you also further the conversation, something that will not happen with a shut-down correction.

Every stage of growing up is magical, full of things young people have never experienced before. You don't have to plan for every stage now. Who knows what you will give your four-year-old granddaughter on her sixteenth birthday? But it does help to think ahead.

For example, Teri D. became a grandmother recently. She thought way ahead.

I had heard about Grandly at a conference I attended when I was not yet a grandmother, but the idea of being strategic about grandparenting caught my attention when I first heard it. My husband and I were thrilled when, shortly thereafter, we first learned we would be grandparents! We knew the day would come, but we didn't expect to be told we would have three grandchildren from three different children and their spouses within nine months!

Suddenly, I had grandchildren's baptisms approaching, and it struck me that I wanted to do more than give a standard gift: booties, stuffed animals, a knitted cap, or a placard with the virtues associated with the baby's name.

I thought about how I could tell these new children of God what a sign of hope they are and how much joy and promise each of them represents. I wanted to tell them how much God loves them and what a good God we have! I wanted to tell them the whole gospel at once: that God sent his Son to redeem us and that Jesus died for us so that we might live. I wanted to tell them how much I have loved them from the moment I knew of their existence and how much I have looked forward to getting to know them even more as they grew. I wanted to tell them that their parents loved them too and that they were doing everything in their power to raise them right. But then my sense of reason tapped my grandmotherly emotions on the shoulder. None of this would make sense to an infant! At least, not now. That is when a strategic grandparent thought hit me.

I asked all of the significant people in each child's life to write notes of encouragement, hope, and love to the newest members of our part of the family of God. The notes were put in a sealed envelope and given to the parents. The parents would be expected to pass them on to the child at an appropriate time in the future, for example, starting school, being confirmed, or at a particularly difficult season in the child's life. The envelopes are awaiting the right time for the child to receive encouragement from aunts, uncles, godparents, and, of course, grandparents.

This idea became more poignant just recently. My mother, their great-grandmother, went to be with the Lord shortly after the births of her great-grandchildren, but she had written them all notes. Her voice will still speak personal encouragement to her great-grandchildren some day in the future when a word of hope and love will be particularly meaningful.

I rejoiced on that day when love and reason kissed! I rejoiced even in the loss of my mother that her voice would make a difference in a day yet to come, and I look forward to hearing what she wrote to those three children when that day comes.

Taking Time to Think

What do you do if your grandchildren live on a different continent? Give up? Quit thinking about your role in their lives? Being an effective grandparent often involves some problem solving. Let's say your grandchildren live in Hawaii, Calgary, London, or New Zealand. It isn't going to be easy to be an effective grandparent, but it is still quite probable that you could be if you work at it.

Jim is the grandfather of a dozen grandchildren. He wrote an article on the need to think through the distance problem:

In 2007, our son and his wife moved to Austria for three years, and they were taking our first grandchild with them! Thus began our adventure as long-distance grandparents. We now have twelve grandchildren, and our desire as Catholic grandparents is to have meaningful relationships with them. Because they live in four time zones and on both sides of the Atlantic, maintaining these relationships across the miles is difficult. However, we have found that a bit of forethought goes a long way.

When planning our visits to our children and grandchildren, we ask ourselves if there is a way to be part of a special event, such as a major birthday or the homecoming of a new baby.

Besides planning when to visit, we think through what we will do while we are there.

We often take a new game to play or book to read with them every day. We look for ways to spend individual time with our grandchildren. Mom and Dad appreciate being able to have a break, so we take the grandchildren for a well-planned outing, or even better, we promote a date night for Mom and Dad. Of course, traveling brings its own set of challenges. Travel costs are an item in our annual budget. We fly when the distance goes beyond our long-drive limit. We've also learned that we need to plan our travel with a bit higher level of personal comfort in mind than before so that we won't arrive exhausted or sleep poorly while we are there. We will need the energy to engage with the children.

We also plan for their visits to us. Spending time together both as a family and one-on-one is a priority when our grandchildren come to visit. Instead of letting things happen, we plan things to do together, such as playing games, cooking, gardening, doing chores, or going on a special outing. Having a kid-friendly house is also conducive to good relationships. We have age-appropriate games, toys, books, sports equipment, and art supplies on hand.

How do we sustain the relationships between visits? Modern technology is a great help. We make our Skype calls when the children will be there to talk with us. We always thank their parents for the digital photos and videos they send, whether on Facebook or by email. Sometimes we make old-fashioned phone calls and send cards or letters. We always tell the grand-kids we are praying for them. We want them to know that we love them. None of this happens by default. It takes thinking and planning ahead.

We have adopted the motto "Think, Pray, and Act Strategi-cally" from Grandly. We have found great joy in not giving up at the first obstacle—or the second or the third. When we get home, we may be jet-lagged or tired, but we also have a great sense of accomplishing our purpose.

There are hundreds of challenges for grandparents to address. Your grandchildren's parents might be divorced. You might have thirty grandchildren. Your grandchildren might live across the street instead of ten hours away. You might have an estranged relationship with your son or daughter. Your financial resources may be thin, or you may be having to put in a lot of time with your own mother in a nursing home.

I know of no magic bullet. I know of no *Universal Grandpar-enting Reference Manual* that addresses everything. Fortunately, you don't face all the challenges there are. You do face some, and many of them are solvable with a bit of strategic think-ing and planning. Some may not be. And that's why you want to learn to pray strategically.

Pray Strategically

Whenever I speak to grandparents, I ask them, "Do you pray for your grandchildren?" Almost all say yes, nod their heads, or show some sign of affirmation. As politely as I can, I then ask, "How do you pray for them?" The most common answer is "Well, uh . . ."

The truth is that most grandparents spend lots of time worrying and little time praying for their grandchildren. Most of us are professional-grade worriers and amateur-grade intercessors, but worrying is a high-grade waste of time. It makes us distressed, irritable, and hopeless.

Admitting the truth that we are mainly worrying is the first step toward effective prayer. The next time you find yourself fretting about something that is going on with one of your grandchildren, stop right there and pray. It doesn't need to be much: "Lord Jesus, be with my granddaughter right now in her trial with . . ." (You might add, "And be with me as well. I don't need the stress of worrying!")

Where are you with prayer? Let's start with those who would answer, "Nowhere! I can't even get started."

The key to becoming more strategic in prayer is to start where you are. Even if you think, "I'm in no place to start," then start by going somewhere else! Don't let yourself be fooled into thinking you can't do that which you can. Where do you start?

Triggers

A trigger, or a switch, is something that initiates a process or reaction. A news article, a video, a radio report, a phone call, a conversation—these can all trigger worrying. Once again, you've pressed your big, red worry button. Your emotions kick into gear, and the worry train starts moving. But with a little rewiring of the brain, you can turn that worry trigger into a prayer trigger. As soon as you recognize, "I am anxious," or you sense the worry train starting to chug, stop and let that be the trigger to pray.

I know someone who gave up chocolate for eight years simply to use it as a prayer trigger. Every time someone offered him chocolate, he turned it down and instead quietly said the Lord's Prayer on behalf of a loved one who needed serious help. Only on Sundays did he accept chocolate, and even then it still worked as a prayer trigger. Over the eight years, he saw almost no change until suddenly, he did. God not only answered his prayers, but God also changed his prayer life and taught him perseverance.

Many grandparents say they don't know how to pray, but they actually do. How many of us say, "Oh, my God!" We are anxious, but OMG is an easy way to start. Add "Help me!" and you have just said a good prayer. Substitute the name of a grandchild for the pronoun "me," and you have said a *very good* prayer.

The Lord's Prayer

But let's look at what you probably already have in your prayer toolbox but may not be using that well: the Lord's Prayer. You don't need to be an articulate intercessor to use the Lord's Prayer well.

A friend of mine is a Minnesota mall walker. From November through March, when the mall opens its doors at 7 a.m., he is the first person in because it is too cold for him to get his exercise walking outdoors. He is one of those who said, "I don't know how to pray." Yet he had everything he needed to put together a great intercession strategy. He needed to combine three simple ingredients: the Lord's Prayer, his daily walk, and his grandchildren's names. He didn't even need to know his grandchildren's needs! I told him, "Start walking. Say, 'Lord, this prayer is for Alyssa, whatever she needs,' and fire off an Our Father." The walk-and-talk method of prayer works. It may not feel as holy as adoration, but walking and talking with God, even in the mall, is a good thing!

Here is an even better example. Henry actually redeemed something he didn't like doing.

Five years ago, I had hip-replacement surgery. To assist with my recovery, the doctor recommended regular exercise, so I began a daily regimen of swimming laps. I hated it but knew I had to do it. It was tedious and boring. My mind would wander, and I'd lose track of the lap count. After a few months of boring, I hit upon the notion of praying for each of our kids and grandkids, devoting a length of the pool for each family member. I could easily keep track of the birth order of my kids and grandkids, so I knew which lap I was on.

I was motivated to pray for them but didn't have a way to do it consistently. This was that. I found a greater motivator than just doing the next lap. I actually wanted to get through my whole family.

I like simple. On the first half of a swim stroke, the prayer is "Jesus." On the second half of the stroke, I pray "Anna" (or Leo or Myriam or Norman). I may get a D for creativity, but I get an A for execution.

Over the years, I have changed the prayer content from time to time. Specific needs come up, like overcoming the flu, so I switch the prayer to "Jesus, heal him." Sometimes I get even more clever and change to a two-stroke rhythmic count: "Jesus, Arnie, help him study."

My wife and I have twenty grandchildren with more on the way. We try to stay well-informed about their lives, but we cannot always keep up with their ever-changing needs. This method of prayer allows me to offer a stripped-down version of intercession for each child, each day. Many opportunities for prayer exist outside the context of a formal daily prayer time. Many exist within the humdrum of daily life.

For me this works swimmingly!

Most of us have things that we do repeatedly. Think of something you do, like ironing, vacuuming, or mowing. There is value in doing those things. Now let's double their value. Think of how you could transform that action by mixing in prayer. You could even get clever about it: "Lord, iron out this problem!"

Here is some good news: You haven't doubled the value of what you did. You have tripled it. How? God will answer your prayer. "What father among you, if his son asks for a fish, will instead of a fish give him a serpent[?]" (Luke 11:11). You can expect God to work in the lives of those you pray for. You ironed, you prayed, and God will act.

But wait! (Oops, this is starting to sound like a TV ad.) There is more good news! You have actually quadrupled your investment. One of the side benefits of prayer is what happens to you. When you pray, you change. Your faith grows. Your anxieties decrease. You will want to become more serious about prayer and start creating good habits of prayer. Prayer will change you as you start to pray for your grandkids.

That's four benefits for the price of one. That's not a bad return on investment.

Fasting

Sometimes we fast in order to petition God and to seek his favor for others. The early Church abstained from food and water to pray more effectively for Paul and Barnabas' ministry (see Acts 13:2-3). They also fasted when choosing leaders for the Church (see 14:23), and David fasted in the hope of saving the life of the baby he had with Bathsheba (see 2 Samuel 12:16-17).

We can choose to sacrifice good and necessary things— food, water, entertainment—as a form of intercession for our grandchildren.

Here is an excellent example of this:

It was December when I had the inspiration to call for a family fast. Like many other cowardly lions, I didn't follow it up right away. But the same prompting from the Lord occurred a few more times. I finally acted when I noted a number of pressing issues among my children and grandchildren. Five out of my six children had lost their jobs or had seen a decline in business or were in a major financial crisis. Important college and career choices were coming up for the grandchildren. In addition, there were health issues for extended family members: prostate cancer, alcohol struggles, mental health concerns, and interpersonal relationship issues.

I proposed to each of my children and their spouses that we have a week of prayer and fasting to seek the Lord's mercy and provision for each other. They all agreed to participate!

The format was this. Each person would fast in some way that would work for him or her. Each day the whole family, grandchildren included, would pray together for that day's specific fast intention. (I made a schedule of the intentions and sent it to everyone.)

We started the week of fasting and prayer at 2 p.m. on Sunday, January 16. Most of the family in our hometown met at my daughter's home. We went over the schedule and committed with each other to the family fast. During the week, I communicated with each family to get a report on how it was going and to give encouragement. Then, on Sunday afternoon, January 23, the families based in Jackson, Michigan, all came to my home, where I had prepared a standing rib roast dinner to celebrate the end of the fast together. Now it was time to see if anything had happened.

One reported twelve new clients that week. We were encouraged to have such a quick and marvelous answer.

After three weeks, another had a new job starting later that month with $22,000 in medical benefits alone. Then another family saw an unusually rapid recovery from surgery on their seven-year-old boy. Then the family member struggling with alcohol quit drinking.

Those answered prayers were great, but more important to me were two other results. First, our family unity was strengthened substantially—a joy for any grandparent. Second, each of us grew in our faith in God, especially the grandchildren. They saw God answer their specific prayers for specific people.

Jesus said to fast and pray. He knew how much good would come from it.

Praying the Long Game

Marion S. sent Grandly another helpful insight on praying the long game. She wrote,

As a child, I thought that when things went well, life was good, and when things went poorly, life was a disaster. As the years have passed, I am now quite aware that short-term setbacks can become long-term benefits. That knowledge impacts how I pray for my grandchildren. They lack the life experiences that display how God can indeed "work all things together for good." But I have seen it! I can pray with the long term in mind. At times, I pray the long game. Playing the long game means you know setbacks aren't the last word. Praying the long game is similar. I know that some things take time to work out, and I have learned to pray patiently.

Praying the long game means praying in faith when I see my grandchildren make choices that are wrong. Remembering some of the temptations I faced in my youth, I now ask God to strengthen my grandchildren to respond well, to learn from their mistakes, and to turn around when they are heading in the wrong direction.

Praying the long game means praying ahead: for future spouses, good careers, and wise decisions on the big issues. It also means I can pray "preventive defense." Long before they face challenges (and I know they will come), I can pray for grace and strength for my grandchildren. I know God loves them even more than I do, and he desires what is best for them. I can pray confidently that God will be there for my grandchildren through their stumbles and failures, and that they will receive the gift of knowing Christ better, experiencing his love more deeply, and growing in character and understanding.

I pray the long game: with confidence, repeatedly, and without anxiety!

And I enjoy it.

The Conversion to Prayer

One of the most common, but seldom described, conversions that happens in people's lives is the conversion to prayer that comes with age. It is fascinating to see. It might even be something that is happening to you already. It is a quiet awakening of a desire to spend more time with the Lord.

I saw older people spending time in my church when I was young. On Saturdays I was ready to do a drive-through confession because I had things to do, games to play, fun to have. But whenever I went to Confession, I always saw some older people who just seemed happy to sit in church and pray.

Is it because the retired finally have time? Are they bored? Or maybe they are desperate? Possibly, but the sweet, gentle conversion to a new, deeper trust in God is common among older people. They enjoy peace in his presence and freedom from a constantly distracted mind. This is a quiet conversion. People don't go around talking about how a bolt from the heavens suddenly changed their lives. They just started praying more and found they liked it.

Maybe you have had a nudge to pray more?

Before we move on to acting strategically, let's note that praying strategically is acting strategically. Your first strategic act could be putting together a prayer list. It might be the names of your grandchildren plus an area where each one could use grace— for good teachers, for example, or good friends, or good health.

Praying well for your grandchildren is one of the most rewarding things any grandparent can do.

Act Strategically

Time

The strategic use of your time is the next most important area after prayer. You need *time* in order to think, to pray, and to act, especially if you are still working, or caring for your own father, or serving on a church committee, or seeing the doctor more often. Our lives are full. "I am too busy!" is a constant refrain. I say it way too often, but then I stop and ask myself what I really mean—after all, I have 168 hours per week, the same as everyone else. For most of us, what it really means is that our priorities aren't clear enough, and so we cannot be peaceful.

If you listened to the radio in the mid-seventies, you certainly heard the song "Cat's in the Cradle" sung by Harry Chapin. It tells of a father who can't get time to be with his son and ends with the son not having time to spend with his father. The dad realizes that his boy has become just like him.

Harry Chapin's wife, Sandy, wrote the song after she heard another song about an old couple looking out the window at a rusted swing and a sandbox. They were reminiscing about the good old days, first, with all the children and, then, with the grandchildren and how it passed and then was all gone.

In 2009, Sandy Chapin was a grandmother, and her focus was on her six grandchildren. As might be expected of the person who wrote "Cat's in the Cradle," she highly valued the time she could spend with them while they were still young. She noted, however, that the eldest of her grandchildren—a granddaughter—had entered the sixth grade in a school where everybody acted like teenagers already. She said,

You have to grab those years. It used to be when I would drive up to the house, she would jump out and run and greet me, and say, "Grandma, what's the project for today?" Because I would always bring some arts and crafts. We'd make Thanksgiving place cards or Christmas tree ornaments. But all through the year, I was always doing projects with them. So now she's answering her email, she's on her cell phone and planning dates, walking around town with her friends, being a grown-up, and doing all the after-school activities. You have to grab that chance when you have it.[2]

Apparently, Sandy Chapin had a strategy for working with her grandchildren when they were young, but she didn't have one for working with them as teenagers. But having a workable set of plans for interacting with your teenage grandchildren is key to successful youth work. And it takes time to develop a strategy because teens are a whole different matter than children. You need to put nursery rhymes on the shelf, next to the baby bottle, and develop a strategy for working with teenagers.

Teens don't climb onto your lap anymore. A new world of distraction has hold of their brains: music, sex, sports, academics, friends, and more. The Tetris game of life just sped up a notch. In a teenager's life, time suddenly becomes far more valuable than it was as a child. That means it will cost you, as a grandparent, more thought and more time if you want to be part of the lives of your teenage grandchildren.

The temptation, however, is to become a passive observer. Go and watch them play soccer.

"Great game, Ellie."

"Thanks, Grandma."

"When is your next game?"

"Tuesday. Gotta get on the team bus. See ya next week?"

"Wouldn't miss it."

What to Do

What's a grandparent of a teenager to do? Conversations with children are simple. Teens are another matter—they are becoming adults. You don't overlap with their world of pizza, pop music, school, and horror movies. They don't overlap with your health issues, 401(k), politics, and obituaries. You have to find the overlap. In the overlap, time is still gold.

If you have a good relationship with your grandchildren, you will know the interests each teenage grandson or granddaughter has. Almost all five-year-olds are happy to read a book with an adult, but there are fewer magic bullets for grandparents of a fourteen-year-old. Classic rock 'n' roll might be of interest to one, but another only likes hip-hop. I gladly went fishing and golfing in my teens, but I had no interest in the NBA. I liked cooking but hated shopping. Some art interested me, but hunting didn't. Teens can have strong interests, but those interests may last only one season. The good news is that it is not that hard to identify their interests if you actually are interested in finding them out!

The easiest way is to ask. Sometimes you might be able to ask directly, "Maria, what activity would be of interest to both of us?" I doubt many teens would be able to give you a long list, but they might suggest a winner now and then. Sometimes you have to ask indirectly, "What would be one thing neither of us would want to do? I'll start: 'Eating salamanders!' Now you!" That might open the door to asking, "So, what do you think we would like to do together?"

Would that work with your granddaughter? Maybe, maybe not. The point is to have her find an activity that would work for both of you. I know one grandmother who took her grandson to the *Messiah* because he liked that kind of music. They had a great discussion afterward about which "song" each considered the best and why. Had my grandmother taken me, I would have been asleep in ten minutes.

You can always do purposeful things with teens: volunteer at a local soup kitchen, orphanage, or retirement home. Few teens would put these on a list of their favorite things to do, but most of them, having done it, will recognize the reward that naturally comes from helping those in need.

Similarly, you can always ask teens for help, especially with technology. Most teens can identify at least five smartphone apps you really should know and use. Helping adults like you is a great way to help teens feel more like adults. (Having said that about smartphones, taking them somewhere that their phones do not run their lives is also a good idea.)

Here are eighteen things to do with a teen:

- Bake homemade bread together.
- Explore a nearby city. Visit the noteworthy, beautiful, historical, or interesting sites.

- Do a corn maze.
- Be a tourist in your own city.
- Do a cathedral tour, noting windows, statues, the location of the baptistery, confessionals, choir loft, etc. When and why was it built, and by whom?
- Write a letter to your senator, bishop, or a new, young, sports professional. (They might respond!)
- Watch an important classic movie after researching why it was important.
- Play "I'll bet that . . ." I'll bet that bird will fly away in less than ten seconds. The next car we'll see is a Ford . . .
- Set up a photo competition for your grandchildren once they have cell phones: first one back here with pictures of a bird, bug, oak tree, SUV, and someone under ten . . .
- Go to a museum.
- Cook a special dinner just for Mom and Dad.
- Take "a pic a day for a week." Exchange them with a grandchild. Have a theme: things important to me, that's weird, or where am I?
- Read a short whodunit, or solve a mystery puzzle together.
- Do a science experiment.
- Each get the same Calvin and Hobbes cartoon book. Choose the funniest among ten cartoons, and say why you think they're funny.
- Volunteer together to help your community.
- Time a sunset from start to finish. How long do you think it will take?
- Change the oil in your car.

Using Your Home

Acting strategically generally involves using what you have on hand to pass on your faith. What do you have on hand? You have a whole toolbox of resources: money, a home, a car, technology, and more.

One of the most powerful tools you have is your home. In sports this is called home-field advantage. In the NFL and the NBA, multiple studies show that the home team wins about 58% of the time. Ink is often wasted on exactly where the advantage lies: crowd noise, fan support, familiarity, travel fatigue, or the intangibles. In any case, in grandparenting, your home-field advantage is significant. The whole environment is yours!

Your home is a tool that almost no youth worker has. Yes, the youth worker has a place to live, but youth workers are not family, and they don't normally bring youth into their homes. You do. Once again, as a strategic grandparent, you have the advantage over an ordinary youth worker, but only if you strategically set up your home, not just so that a two-year-old is safe, but so that a ten-year-old wants to engage the environment and that environment is set up to pass on your faith.

Walls

Your home has an influence on everyone who comes into it. Your home speaks. Go into your friends' homes, and look at what they have in their bookcases or on their mantelpieces. You may be surprised at what a bookcase tells you.

What you hang on the walls of your home, display on your coffee table, or post on your refrigerator is important.

For example, Pope St. John Paul II may not be your uncle nor St. Therese your great-great-aunt, but if they were models who shaped your life, you could consider hanging pictures of them on a wall in your hallway. Your grandchildren, with their natural curiosity, will probably take notice. When they see an unfamiliar picture, they will probably pause, or they might ask, "Who is that?" Or you might ask them, "Who do you think that is?" These questions can be the springboard to a great conversation.

Additionally, periodically rotating who is on your wall of fame will multiply your conversation opportunities. Change the channel every once in a while, and see what happens.

Reproductions of great religious paintings also speak. At a certain age, art comes alive, especially if you can explain what a painting "says" with its layout, colors, positioning, or lighting. *The Angelus* by Jean-François Millet is located in the Musée d'Orsay in Paris. It depicts a man and a woman who have paused in their work in the middle of a field to pray the Angelus. The idea for the painting came to Millet because he remembered that when his grandmother heard the church bell ringing, she would have them stop work to say the Angelus for those who had died.

Grandma Millet did the right thing! Today we have a phenomenal work of art that has inspired many to stop what they are doing and briefly pray because she did that with her grandson. We also have a story we can tell our grandchildren about a great work of art.

Stained glass windows in a church once served a similar purpose as your wall of art. Those windows weren't there only to let in a bit of light or to add some color. Most people in earlier times couldn't read. A catechism or a Bible was of little value to an illiterate audience, especially if it was written in Latin and you spoke Anglo-Saxon. But a window showing Moses with the Ten Commandments could be used to tell the story of how God gave the commandments to his people and then used them as a means of instructing children in how to keep those commandments.

You probably don't have a stained glass window, but you can put up some religious art.

Music

What youth worker doesn't understand the powerful influence of music on young people? Who hasn't said, "I can't get that song out of my head"? Why do we sing lullabies to children? They work! Why do we have heroic music in *Star Wars* movies? It elicits the right emotions in action sequences that otherwise would be flat.

In your home, you own the environment, and your background music can have foreground results. Today you can call up the kinds of songs you want to hear directly on Spotify or though Alexa or Siri. This Christmas, ask Alexa to play Christian Christmas songs. Fill your house with "Joy to the World." Your grandchildren will hear "Frosty the Snowman" elsewhere.

You don't have to remodel your house to speak volumes. It probably already can!

Books

My grandparents had few books and no bookcases, but I knew people who had them. Most of the books were dusty, but some people had a library full of kids' books. They had bright covers and eye-catching art right at eye level: forty inches from the ground. Books by Dr. Seuss were lodged below books about Tom Sawyer and Nancy Drew. St. Francis had a spot next to *The Babe Ruth Story*. I wasn't raised in a family that was big on reading, but eventually I did read most of the books I saw on my friend's bookshelves, just because I saw them on those bookshelves.

As a boy, I couldn't see the books on the top shelf, and they had titles that wouldn't interest me until years later. *Crime and Punishment* and *Brideshead Revisited* certainly weren't attention grabbing to a young teen, but when I was tall enough, I read the titles and eventually read the books.

A bookshelf can make a difference, especially if that's where you store the books you read to your grandchildren when they visit. They will want to move up a shelf sooner or later. When they do, you can always ask, "Do you think you're ready?" That might make them more ready!

Grandad's bookshelf might be exactly what a restless young man needs to fire his imagination and make him want to be like a *Young Abe Lincoln*. Have you considered expanding your library? There are oodles of children's and teens' books that recount the stories of Bible heroes and Catholic saints. Start with the ones you know. Or even better, work your way through the Litany of Saints:

Mary the Mother of God, Michael, Gabriel, Raphael, John the Baptist, Joseph, Peter, Paul, Andrew, James, John, Thomas, James, Philip, Bartholomew, Matthew, Simon, Thaddeus, Matthias, Barnabas, Luke, Mark, Stephen, Lawrence, Vincent, Fabian, Sebastian, John, Paul, Cosmas, Damian, Gervase, Protase, Silvester, Gregory, Ambrose, Augustine, Jerome, Martin, Nicholas, Anthony, Benedict, Bernard, Dominic, Francis, Mary Magdalene, Agatha, Lucy, Agnes, Cecilia, Catharine, Anastasia.

That's a starter list of fifty-two, and it may not include your granddaughter's patron saint. Or, if you have a grandson preparing for Confirmation, you could offer to do some research together to find the saint that would be most inspiring to him.

Grandparents can provide a library that no youth worker can.

Money

Speaking of gold, what's in your wallet? Probably not actual gold, but money, credit cards, and photos of your grandchildren. There is a connection here.

A grandparent can seriously outperform a youth worker fiscally. Youth worker: "Hey Tim, I have tickets to *Spiderman Returns, Once More, Again, Part Two.* It's the sequel to the prequel's second sequel. Wanna go?" Grandpa: "Hey Tim, how about you join us for an Alaskan cruise as our graduation present to you? Bring a friend." OK, most of us can't do that, but do you remember how the strategic grandparenting idea began? I was observing a grandfather who unstrategically used his money as a birthday gift. Money itself isn't strategic, but how you use it is, especially with teens.

If you offer your six-year-old grandson a choice between a fifty-dollar bill or an ice cream cone, you will keep your money and lose your ice cream. If you offer to send your sixteen-year-old granddaughter on a two-hundred-dollar weekend retreat or offer her two hundred dollars in cash, she will likely take the money and control her destiny. Nevertheless, it is your money and your choice about how you invest it. Offering to pay for the retreat is more strategic than giving cash.

George is a grandfather who has a wonderful relationship with his daughter, her husband, and their three children. His thirteen-year-old grandson and his ten-year-old granddaughter are now old enough to attend a Christian summer camp. Because he prefers to use his money for good things, he eagerly offered to pay the cost of the camp for them. His daughter and son-in-law gladly accepted the offer and made the necessary arrangements for his grandchildren to attend.

As with many Christian summer camps, this one helped them become more familiar with God's word through a Bible study every morning. His grandchildren were taught how to have better prayer lives and to pray more often. They learned how to live with others, putting others' needs above their own, and of course, they learned the basic skills that are a part of a camping experience—like how to roast marshmallows and not do stupid things with fire!

After the camp, parents were invited to bring their children to a post-camp testimonial meeting. George wasn't present, but he got the full report from his daughter. She and her husband were proud when both of their children, unprompted, went forward at the time to share about camp and spoke in front of three hundred people. His grandson told those in attendance that he had asked the Holy Spirit for the gift of discernment because he wanted to be able to help other people. (George laughed when he heard this and said, "It takes the gift of discernment to pray for discernment!") His granddaughter requested the gift of prayer. (He laughed again and said, "So she prayed for the gift of prayer?")

He told me, "Just hearing from my daughter about the children's experiences would have been enough for me, but then my grandchildren called me and thanked me for helping them go to summer camp. They told me about how they learned to know and serve God better. Money well spent, I say!"

How many grandparents have helped send their grandchildren to summer camps or on mission trips? Lots, and they made a great investment.

Doc and Judy have nine children and forty grandchildren. They wanted their grandchildren to connect with other Christians their own age. They saw the value of sending them out to see the wide world of faith in Belgium and Belfast, Denver and Detroit, London and Lansing. Their children—the parents of the grandchildren—agreed.

Most of their children can afford to send their children on things like mission trips, but not all of them can. Doc and Judy pooled birthday and Christmas money to send their grandson Kyle on a retreat.

They had him come over afterward to tell them how it went. They also invited his younger cousin John (next on their list) to join them.

We asked Kyle for one thing he learned from this year's YES Retreat that he would like to share with Jonny. He answered, "You can only find real joy, joy that satisfies, by putting God first, by serving Jesus Christ. The things of the world don't do it."

Our grandson spoke the truth with conviction to our other grandson. We got double our money's worth out of this year's investment. It was a holy investment, and it bore compound interest because one grandchild influenced another in his faith journey!

If you have money available to spend on your grandchildren, it probably means you learned how to use it wisely and to spend it carefully. Keep it up!

Skills

You might know the distinctive handwriting style of your father, mother, siblings, and friends. I have kept some letters from my grandfather, and when I handle them, they communicate more than simply the words on the paper.

One of the saddest developments in modern education is that children are no longer being taught cursive writing. Keyboard skills are much more valuable today, and that means most children born since 2010 won't be able to read cursive. For your grandchildren who can read cursive, however, a handwritten letter might provide a much deeper connection and be a more significant form of communicating love than it was in your day. Yes, voice to text will be more efficient, but your distinctive, personality-reflecting cursive script brings you with it.

Grampa Louis wrote to us:

There's something special about getting a handwritten letter. It was more common when I was young, but now a handwritten letter is a rare treat.

I find that a letter allows me to express myself more accurately and completely than a phone call. I used to send letters to my own children who were still living at home! Now I send letters to my grandkids. Typically, I write a little about some experience I've had and encourage them in their walk with the Lord. Below, I have shared a letter that I wrote to one of my grandchildren.

Dear Maggie:

Hello and Happy Birthday again! I just wanted to follow up on the little hand-carved, wooden man I gave you for your birthday. It has a special significance for me.

I found the little statue in a small shop in Cuenca, Ecuador, high in the Andean Mountains. (I lived in South America working as a Peace Corps Volunteer from 1964 to 1966. My job was to run a medical clinic in a poor neighborhood.) The people in Ecuador are mostly poor, and they don't have lots of "stuff" to worry about. But they have a faith in God that makes them content with their lives and gives them hope for their future.

During my time in Ecuador, I collected locally carved or hand-made wooden and woven goods. The little man was one of my favorites. When I saw this little man, it reminded me of Jesus the Good Shepherd. He has the staff. He has a little sheepdog next to his side. He appears to be intently looking out for something or someone—me!

Back in 1966, I didn't know the exact path for my life since my whole life was before me, but Jesus knew. I picked up this "Good Shepherd" back then, not quite realizing that the Good Shepherd had already picked me up. I want you to have it so that you can be reassured that he will lead you, guide you, and protect you exactly as his word says and like he did for me!

Writing letters seems to be a lost art these days, but it really takes no special skills. You can do it: all you need is a message to communicate. Every Wednesday of Lent, for example, you could write a letter about a different and significant way you have experienced God's grace. By the time Lent is over, you will have covered seven of your most significant experiences. You can finish by noting that the eighth will come in heaven, and it will be perfect.

Okay, writing letters may not be your thing. What is? Here are twenty skills you could use to bond with your grandchildren:

- calligraphy
- fishing
- floral design
- glass etching
- hairstyling and cutting

- jewelry making
- knitting, needlepoint, crochet, embroidery
- leatherwork
- metalwork and smithing
- instrument playing, singing
- origami
- quilting
- rope making, knot tying
- scrapbooking
- sewing
- sports
- stone crafts
- swimming or sailing
- upholstery
- whittling

You almost certainly have some specific skills to use in relationship building. It could be a doorway to passing on your faith. If you can whistle while you work, you can probably talk about your faith while you whittle.

Technology

Whenever we do Grandly seminars, we ask people about technology. Some grandparents are fairly up to speed. Their active vocabulary includes not just Facebook and Google, but FaceTime, WhatsApp, Twitter, Snapchat, Skype, and Instagram.

Some know or even use Twitch and Hangouts. Some hear these words and just say, "What?"

There is a great video on YouTube from 1936.[3] (It's a "movie reel" that was shown in theaters—there was no television.) In it, AT&T introduces the first rotary-dial telephone—an upgrade from working with an operator to place a call. Prior to the new rotary phone, people had to lift the earpiece from the rocker, double tap the rocker to contact the switchboard operator, tell her whom they wanted to speak to, and then wait while she put the call through.

In the video, an eleven-year-old girl demonstrates how to use the rotary dial, what a ringtone is, and what a busy signal sounds like. AT&T clearly knew how challenging it is to upgrade your technology but wanted to show that even a child could learn to do it.

Don't let the fear of new technology determine your relationship with your grandchildren. If you can google it, you can probably learn to do it.

D. Waters is the grandfather of five grandchildren, and recently, he ran into a problem:

We were having four of our grandchildren stay at our house for five days. We drove to their house, packed everything they needed, and brought them to our home fifty miles away.

I wanted to maintain the pattern of prayer that my son and daughter-in-law had set for them. I knew that establishing good spiritual habits requires consistency. They used a daily devotional that had a story for young children, a short Bible verse to be memorized, and, finally, a simple prayer that they could say together.

When we unpacked the car, we found the daily devotional somehow had been left behind. Suddenly, in order to maintain what my son and daughter-in-law had fought so hard to achieve, I was facing one hundred miles round-trip. Just the thought was depressing.

Call it an inspiration, a lead, a nudge from the Holy Spirit. I went inside and fired up my computer. In a minute I was searching the internet for children's Christian devotionals. Up popped multiple options to choose from: free and online. Hooray for modern technology!

I chose one that suited my needs and came up with a week's worth of material in about ten minutes. I had a great week seeing our grandchildren growing from strength to strength and never missing a beat.

I thank God for Christians who help other Christians through modern technology.

I especially like Grandly.org, because it is an "internet" of grandparents helping grandparents do grand things for grandchildren.

"Mr. Granddad" is one grandfather who was even more involved with his grandchildren electronically. Mr. Schillings retired from classroom teaching fourteen years ago, but he returned to teaching as "Mr. Granddad," a homeschool teacher for his grandchildren.

Our four children are all married and are living in four different states: a son in Wisconsin and daughters in Ohio, Idaho, and Arizona. Our twenty-four grandchildren are expanding the spread: Virginia, Michigan, Washington, and Montana—and further spreading looks likely. Despite living far away from most of my grandkids, I found a way of staying close to them and having a positive impact on their lives.

Most of our twenty-four grandchildren were homeschooled. It was a natural transition for me to teach them history, government, and economics via iChat and then Skype on a regular schedule.
The junior high itinerary included lessons, assignments, and discussions. I also added Bible lessons and prayer. Because so many were the same age, I connected our grandchildren with their cousins "in class." I used history and economics books that were very well done and interesting and that came from a clear Christian perspective.

By the time each child was sixteen, our sessions either ended or decreased because nearly all of them began taking online or junior college classes before moving on with their education. My grandkids were now ready for the next step. Not only did they have a well-rounded secular education, but they also had a solid foundation in Christian values and thinking. The time we had prior to college was doubly important because they attended colleges that were unsupportive of Christianity or even hostile to it, in one case. Our grandchildren needed to be well equipped in their faith to stand up to opposition. Fortunately, so far, our grandchildren have proven strong in their beliefs.

Teaching is about preparing children for adulthood. My background in education enabled me to do a lot for my grandchildren to aid in that preparation. Learning to use modern technology made me an effective long-distance teacher: "Mr. Granddad."

Don't be afraid of technology. You don't need to learn everything, but do find one new technology you can use to pass on your faith more effectively. You only need to learn how to use the right app for you, whether FaceTime, Skype, or WhatsApp, to be able to see and talk to your grandchildren anywhere on the planet.

In this chapter, we delved into the *how* question. How do you think, pray, and act strategically? We hope you have moved from an aim to a game, from an intention to a strategy, and that you are ready to do grandparenting grandly.

CHAPTER 5

DO IT GRANDLY

Grandparenting?

By now you should be accustomed to that word, even if your computer spell-checker puts squiggly red lines under it. You won't find it in the major dictionaries yet. Like many words, the noun form came first. The English word "grandparent" only appeared in 1830. The verb "parenting" only appears in 1959. "Verbing" nouns—from "grandparent" to "grandparenting," for example—is now becoming a thing.

Grandly?

Our work, Grandly, began with only a concept: helping ordinary grandparents become strategic grandparents. We didn't have a name or a website. One day, doing a random search, I saw that grandly.org was still available as a website. Grandly, I thought? Is it a word? I looked in the dictionary. Yes, it's an adverb. An adverb? I briefly thanked my elementary school teachers when I remembered that adverbs describe how something is done: quickly, lively, gladly, strategically. We had just settled on the phrase "think, pray, and act strategically." We were developing *how to* help grandparents. We needed adverbs! Grandly isn't a commonly used one, but we are doing our best to make it so.

The Oxford English Dictionary defines "grandly" as, "in a proud, impressive, or ambitious manner."[4] We use grandly in a positive sense: doing something grandly is doing it well. In 2017 we held our first seminar. We called it "Do It Grandly" simply to make the point that when it comes to grandparenting, it is worth striving for excellence. "If you are doing grandparenting, do it grandly."

This book contains much of the content we have developed for our *Do It Grandly* seminar. I hope the book has inspired you to be a strategic grandparent, but keep in mind that this is only a book. A book is great, but a book about a tour of Europe is not a tour of Europe. Experiencing something is quite different than reading about it. The *Do It Grandly* seminar is experience oriented. It converts and motivates; it doesn't just inform. The seminar includes inspiring talks and personal stories, but even more importantly, it includes face-to-face discussions during which grandparents talk together about their own grandchildren. Everyone gets to share about trials and successes in grandparenting in an atmosphere of hope and encouragement. No one goes home without at least a few takeaways and a boatload of hope.

You can get more information on how to sponsor a *Do It Grandly* seminar by emailing us at grandly.org@gmail.com. The seminar lasts four to five hours. We provide the speakers, materials, and everything a parish, organization, or institution needs to put on a life-changing seminar for any group of grandparents.

Conclusion

Most people don't think the way I do about either grandparents or youth workers. They don't see grandparents as potentially effective youth workers. "Grandparents aren't young, they aren't cool, and they don't understand youth. How can they be youth workers?"

I hope you now see how wrong that thinking is.

The Church needs youth workers, but what it really needs is many more youth workers in the position you are in. The Church needs grandparents working with youth.

This book is not about you. It is about young people. Our work in Grandly will not be measured by how many grandparents receive hope, vision, and youth-work skills. It will be measured by how many young people become the leaders the Church needs over the next seventy years. Grandly is simply a network of grandparents who inspire each other in this great task.

When I think of today's grandparents, I see what potentially could be the most effective missionary movement in Church history. The massive baby-boomer generation has begun its grandparenting years. Baby boomers are retiring at an average of ten thousand *per day*. Over the next twenty years, an estimated seventy million American baby boomers will retire. What would happen if we raised up just 0.1 percent of them to be missionaries to their grandchildren? That would be seventy thousand youth workers, all over the age of fifty-five, who could easily affect a million youth. They could have an unprecedented impact on a generation of young people. If they do that, it could be the loudest and longest boom of the baby-boomer generation. These grandparents would be hope-filled witnesses more committed and better equipped than any youth workers ever.

Grandly was founded to help grandparents become missionaries. You don't need to go to Africa, Asia, or Alaska. You can be missionaries to your own grandchildren, right where you are.

Every *Do It Grandly* seminar features a young person telling about their "missionary" grandma or grandpa. A young woman from Michigan State University told this story:

Growing up, I was a nominal Christian. I had a basis for Christianity—semi-regularly attending church with my family and Sunday school classes. In reality, I didn't have a relationship with Christ, which was apparent in my words and actions. Throughout middle and high school, I was very self-conscious and saw little purpose for my life. Starting college, I was interested in living life my own way—including who I was friends with, how late we would stay out, or what we would be doing on those late nights. I quickly found a group of friends in the dorms who wanted to party with me.

However, in November of my freshman year, my grandma suddenly got sick. I wasn't sure if she would recover. During the final three weeks when she was in the hospital, I had lots of time to reflect on her life. I recalled the subtle conversations we'd had about God. He was her motivation for kindness, truth, and a gentle strength. When she caught wind of dishonesty or cruelty, my grandma's words were simply, "That's not how we treat people." She lived the gospel through speech and action, teaching me about authentic Christianity. My life consisted of self-absorption, partying, and foolish behavior. When she died, I started to pray broken and honest prayers for the first time. My grandma and I were very close, and her passing led me to examine my life. I realized all the lies I was caught up in, which had started eating away at me.

As I thought about my grandma and her life, I decided I wanted to model mine on hers.

I had gotten really close to one of my suite mates at college, and she attended prayer meetings with a Christian group on campus called University Christian Outreach. Suddenly, I was curious about it, so I decided to tag along one week, and then I kept going after that. I began to choose God more and more. My "yes" didn't happen in one moment but was a series of small "yeses" over the rest of that year.

That probably wouldn't have happened without my grandma's death calling me to act. Her decision to follow Christ clearly led to my own decision to do likewise.

Think about it! This young woman's testimony was that her grandmother modeled a way of life that she didn't follow while her grandmother lived. It became the model she followed, however, once her grandma died. Grandma is almost certainly rejoicing in heaven today because God numbered her days exactly—for the sake of her granddaughter. Keep in mind that Grandma didn't know how this would all turn out; she didn't know any of this while she was alive. But her granddaughter is now leading a Bible study and inviting others into the great adventure of living as one of Christ's disciples. Only God knows how much Grandma's influence will ripple outward through the next generation.

It is time to think differently: what if the most important mission in your whole life is about to begin right now? If you engage that mission, it will make a difference in the lives of your grandchildren, and it will make a difference in the lives of everyone both you and they touch.

Think about it—you could end life as a missionary. That is thinking strategically.

It's time to pray differently. "Lord, make me a missionary to my own grandchildren, for their good and for your glory." That is praying strategically.

It's time to act differently. Make a decision to implement one idea that you have read about in this book. It's time to do mission. That is acting strategically.

If you do these things, you will be one of seventy thousand grandparents who are starting to think, pray, and act strategically. Finish your race well. Do the most important thing you have ever done in your life. Go make some waves. You are on a great—no, a grand—mission.

If you are going to do grandparenting, do it GRANDLY!

APPENDIX A

HELP US HELP YOU

The Website

The main mode of activity for Grandly, The Strategic Grand-parents Club, is our website: www.grandly.org. You can help us help you by joining on the Grandly website. Along with interesting posts and articles, you will get a short, interesting stimulus to think, pray, and act strategically in passing on your faith via email on the first and fifteenth of the month.

Where else can you find an article on how to initiate a conversation with a twelve-year-old boy? Or how to find a great website for a Christian teenage girl? Or how about this point: what's weird about a teenage brain? That article explains many of your head-scratchers. Well-trained and effective youth workers who understand youth and youth culture have written about those topics for Grandly.

Strategic grandparents contribute their ideas too. Many of them have written articles and short posts describing what they have done as strategic grandparents and why it has worked. Those articles and ideas inspire other grandparents to do something similar but different, to adapt an idea to their own situation. It is a grandparent's "Aha!" or "Wow!" moment. The

Grumpy Grandpa article about overcoming negativity sparked a grandmother to begin texting a message of encouragement to her teenage granddaughter every day.

The website is easy to navigate and has a simple menu: "Get Help" and "Give Help." The Get Help menu gives you access to all the articles, with a search option that allows you to search any term to find an article on that topic. Search "Christmas" or "boys" or "technology," and you will get help. Under Get Help, you can also find out how to host a seminar in your church or for your organization. You can also request a speaker or access our videos.

But you can also Give Help! You could write an article for us, especially on some topics we haven't covered. Our writer's guidelines are on the site. You can pray for us. The site also has a list of things we need—maybe you have time or the business expertise we are looking for. And yes, you can contribute financially. Our Grandly office is supported exclusively by our readers.

Grandly Clubs

Ongoing support happens wherever at least two or three grandparents continue to gather after a seminar to share ideas, discuss articles, and pray for their grandchildren. Groups of strategic grandparents can be the most active and effective way of staying on task. You have friends. They have grandchildren. You all have a mission. We can give you helpful ideas on how to make a Strategic Grandparents Club work. A meeting starts with donuts and coffee and finishes with intercession for your grandchildren. In between, you might discuss things as complicated as the effects of postmodernism on education or as simple as books worth reading with your grandchildren.

What's in a Logo?

What do you see when you look closely at the Grandly logo? You should at least see a "g." The "g" is for grandparents.

If you look more closely at the "g," you will see that it is comprised of an "s" for strategic and a "c" on top of it for club. The Strategic Grandparents Club is in the center of a larger "c" representing your children's children, the mission field we are trying to reach through The Strategic Grandparents Club.

Why is it green? Psalm 92 tells us. It says of the righteous, "They still bring forth fruit in old age, / they are ever full of sap and green" (92:14). Yes, it may be the autumn of your life, but that's when a tree produces apples.

TWENTY-FIVE VIRTUES WORTH INSTILLING IN YOUNG PEOPLE

This is just a checklist, but it might give you some ideas! Circle the virtues that you already know your grandchildren should work on.

- ✓ charity
- ✓ commitment
- ✓ compassion
- ✓ contentment
- ✓ cooperation
- ✓ courage
- ✓ empathy
- ✓ faith
- ✓ forgiveness
- ✓ generosity
- ✓ graciousness
- ✓ gratitude
- ✓ honesty
- ✓ hope
- ✓ humility
- ✓ justice
- ✓ kindness
- ✓ loyalty
- ✓ meekness
- ✓ patience
- ✓ peace
- ✓ perseverance
- ✓ prudence
- ✓ respect
- ✓ tact
- ✓ temperance
- ✓ zeal

A BRIEF OUTLINE OF THE CONTENTS OF THE *CATECHISM OF THE CATHOLIC CHURCH*

Introduction

God created us to be happy with him forever.
We can know God or resist knowing God.
God reveals himself to us.
The full revelation of God is in Jesus and is handed on in Tradition and Sacred Scripture.

Part One: The Creed

I Believe in God the Father Almighty, Creator of Heaven and Earth.
I Believe in Jesus Christ, the Only Son of God.
I Believe in the Holy Spirit.
I Believe in the Holy Catholic Church.
I Believe in the Forgiveness of Sins.

I Believe in the Resurrection of the Body.
I Believe in Life Everlasting.

Part Two: The Sacraments

The Sacrament of Baptism
The Sacrament of Confirmation
The Sacrament of the Eucharist
The Sacrament of Reconciliation
The Sacrament of the Anointing of the Sick
The Sacrament of Holy Orders
The Sacrament of Matrimony
Other Liturgical Celebrations

Part Three: The Ten Commandments

I am the LORD your God. You shall have no other gods before
me. You shall not make for yourself a graven image; you shall
not bow down to them or serve them.
You shall not take the name of the LORD your God in vain.
Remember the Sabbath day, to keep it holy.
Honor your father and your mother.
You shall not kill.
You shall not commit adultery.
You shall not steal.
You shall not bear false witness against your neighbor.
You shall not covet your neighbor's wife.
You shall not covet your neighbor's goods.

Part Four: Prayer

What Is Prayer?
Types of Prayer
Common Ways to Pray
The Lord's Prayer

NOTES

1. Michael Shaughnessy, ed., *A Concise Catholic Catechism* (London: Burns & Oates, 2002), paragraph 302.

2. Sandy Chapin, interview by Carl Wiser, *Songwriter Interviews*, January 7, 2009, https://www.songfacts.com/blog/interviews/sandy-chapin.

3. AT&T Tech Channel, "AT&T Archives: Introduction to the Dial Telephone," YouTube video, 1:23, May 30, 2012, https://www.youtube.com/watch?v=uaQm30DDHL8.

4. *Oxford English Dictionary*, s.v. "grandly," https://www.lexico.com/en/definition/grandly.